GLORIOUS 39

Stephen Poliakoff, born ir
appointed writer in residence at the National Theatre for
1976 and the same year won the *Evening Standard*'s Most
Promising Playwright Award for *Hitting Town* and *City
Sugar*. He has also won a BAFTA Award for the Best
Single Play for *Caught on a Train* in 1980, the *Evening
Standard*'s Best British Film Award for *Close My Eyes* in
1992, The Critics' Circle Best Play Award for *Blinded by
the Sun* in 1996 and the Prix Italia and the Royal
Television Society Best Drama Award for *Shooting the Past*
in 1999. His plays and films include *Clever Soldiers* (1974),
The Carnation Gang (1974), *Hitting Town* (1975), *City
Sugar* (1975), *Heroes* (1975), *Strawberry Fields* (1977),
Stronger than the Sun (1977), *Shout Across the River* (1978),
American Days (1979), *The Summer Party* (1980), *Bloody
Kids* (1980), *Caught on a Train* (1980), *Favourite Nights*
(1981), *Soft Targets* (1982), *Runners* (1983), *Breaking the
Silence* (1984), *Coming in to Land* (1987), *Hidden City*
(1988), *She's Been Away* (1989), *Playing with Trains* (1989),
Close My Eyes (1991), *Sienna Red* (1992), *Century* (1994),
Sweet Panic (1996), *Blinded by the Sun* (1996), *The Tribe*
(1997), *Food of Love* (1998), *Talk of the City* (1998),
Remember This (1999), *Shooting the Past* (1999), *Perfect
Strangers* (2001) for which he won the Dennis Potter
Award at the 2002 BAFTAs and Best Writer and Best
Drama at the Royal Television Society Awards, and *The
Lost Prince* (2003), winner of three Emmy Awards in 2005
including Outstanding Mini Series, *Friends and Crocodiles*
(2006) and *Gideon's Daughter* (also 2006), which won two
Golden Globes and a Peabody Award in 2007. His most
recent work for the BBC includes *Joe's Palace*, *Capturing
Mary* and *A Real Summer* (all 2007).

by the same author

STEPHEN POLIAKOFF PLAYS: ONE
Clever Soldiers; Hitting Town; City Sugar; Shout Across the River;
American Days; Strawberry Fields

STEPHEN POLIAKOFF PLAYS: TWO
Breaking the Silence; Playing with Trains; She's Been Away;
Century

STEPHEN POLAKOFF PLAYS: THREE
Caught on a Train; Coming in to Land; Close My Eyes

Friends and Crocodiles/Gideon's Daughter (screenplays)

Joe's Palace/A Real Summer/Capturing Mary (screenplays)

The Lost Prince (screenplay)

Perfect Strangers (screenplay)

Remember This

Shooting the Past (screenplay)

Sweet Panic/Blinded by the Sun

Talk of the City

GLORIOUS 39

Stephen Poliakoff

With a Q and A with the author

Methuen Drama

Published by Methuen Drama 2009

10 9 8 7 6 5 4 3 2

Methuen Drama
A & C Black Publishers Limited
36 Soho Square
London W1D 3QY
www.methuendrama.com

ISBN: 978 1 408 12226 6

A CIP catalogue record for this book is available from
the British Library

Typeset by Country Setting, Kingsdown, Kent
Printed and bound in Great Britain by CPI Cox and Wyman,
Reading, Berkshire

Contents

Q and A with the Author

MARK DUDGEON We're here to discuss *Glorious 39*. It's over ten years since your last film for cinema release and, in recent times, you've been a vociferous advocate of writing and directing for TV, so what prompted the return to the cinema?

STEPHEN POLIAKOFF I think what moved me away from cinema was the distribution situation for British films in this country, which got particularly bad in the 1990s. *Close my Eyes*, the most successful film I've made to date, despite winning a Best British Film Award and doing better business in its first few weeks than a lot of big Hollywood movies in London, still could not get on the major circuit in Britain. And then the film reached an awful lot of people through television and was shown many times on Channel 4, so when I made *Shooting the Past* and *Perfect Strangers* and then *The Lost Prince*, which was quite a successful piece, I thought is this worse than making cinema? And the answer is no, because you are making films with total creative control and you're able to do quite difficult things. I'd been thinking of returning to the cinema for at least five or six years but I wanted to return with a subject that I felt had a realistic chance of getting good distribution and reaching a number of people around the world but that I also felt passionate about. When *The Lost Price* won the Emmy Awards, people said 'Come on, come back to the cinema', but nothing I was offered really fired me up. And it was only when *Gideon's Daughter* won the Golden Globes with Bill Nighy and Emily Blunt that I really thought seriously about returning to the cinema. And so *Glorious 39* came about and I found I'd had an idea that I did feel passionate about. At the back of my mind I'd always wanted to make a suspenseful thriller but I wanted it to have heart and to feel fresh, because I felt that there was no point making something that was like something else. And then the right conditions for making the film came about: I had an idea, BBC Films was very enthusiastic about developing it, the UK Film Council and then Momentum came in to distribute it, we got a really great cast together and suddenly there was a perfect storm for making a film. And *Glorious 39* is the result.

MD   So let's go back if we can to the original idea that you had for the film. How long ago did that come to you?

SP   I think the idea originated about three or four years ago when I was thinking what a close-run thing it was that I was here. Because my parents were both born before the First World War and didn't have children until they were nearly in their forties I felt in touch with the 1930s. So it has always been part of my upbringing really, what a close-run thing it was that the British government didn't do a deal with Hitler. After writing *Capturing Mary*, which was quite a dark story with a spooky, visceral centre, I felt that was quite an interesting area for me to build on. I've always liked thrillers and films that satisfy in a suspenseful way but that also have things carefully worked out and make psychological and emotional sense. And that's quite a difficult thing to achieve. I felt that this was an ambitious thing to do because there are not many thrillers like that. Inevitably, all thrillers are compared with Hitchcock, who was such a great genius, and so it's impossible to compare any modern film with that. Nevertheless, I wanted to attempt something in that tradition or like another of my favourite movies, Polanski's *Rosemary's Baby*, where you have that building of subtle suspense. And so the ambition to try to make a film like that with this historical background came together after I'd made *Capturing Mary*. A lot of the research had been building up over the years as I got more and more interested in this period and began reading diaries: Channon's diary; the diary of Duff Cooper – who was a cabinet minister against appeasement; the diary of John Colville – who was Private Secretary to both Chamberlain and Churchill. So diaries were great because people don't know what's going to happen the next day, they're not writing in retrospect, however much they might have touched them up to make them read better. There is an authenticity of sorts about them and so if you can get your hands on a diary there's always something that suddenly opens a door and you feel you're there. There are also some fantastic books about the build-up to war. One of the best is *Troublesome Young Men* by Lynne Olson. It's a compulsive read about the young men clustering around Churchill and trying to bring down Chamberlain.

MD   The film is released around the same time as the seventieth anniversary of the outbreak of the war; how important to your process in writing, the selection of material, and the release and distribution of the film is this anniversary?

SP   I didn't write the film because of the anniversary, but it is a powerful reminder that it isn't that long ago that these things happened. Christopher Lee, who begins and finishes the film, was very much there and remembers it very vividly, as does Muriel Pavlow, who plays the older Anne in the film. And if we hadn't confronted Hitler, I wouldn't be here and my family wouldn't be here, and that was one of the most powerful motivations for making the film.

MD   Did you feel as a result a different burden of responsibility to tell the story accurately and show people what it was really like?

SP   I think that cinema is not the right place to teach history. I think that television history is very good and is a powerful way of doing popular history. But for *Glorious 39*, it has to be first and foremost an entertainment; this is what Hitchcock always said and it is true that you try to engage people on the most visceral level. Within that you are trying to give it a reality as well, so I didn't invent any historical facts or detail other than obviously the murders that take place. But what is definitely true is the main thrust of the story, that the Secret Service were monitoring the phone calls and spying on the people who were particularly against appeasement and certainly the group of young Tory MPs who were trying to bring Chamberlain down. And so there's a lot of truth in the fabric of the story and definitely in the big set-pieces like people putting their pets down.

Because people feared that they were going to be bombed really heavily, they either left town or were evacuated and didn't want to take their pets with them, or they thought that it was humane to put their pets down. So one went from these golden weeks of parties – the aristocracy had been holding some of the greatest parties of the twentieth century, and if you were travelling through London you would have been aware of these going on, seeing people driving up to Holland House in the middle of London and in Regent's Park – to then, three or four weeks later, travelling through the same city and seeing piles of dead animals everywhere. There was an extraordinary change within a few weeks and for me as a film-maker and dramatist that was a really interesting way of conveying how easy it would have been to manipulate people.

MD   The bonfire of the pets in one of the London parks is an incredibly powerful image of that destruction, and it's Alexander who says, 'How have we got to this?'

SP   One of the tragedies of history is that by the end of the 1930s the British political class exaggerated how strong Germany was, as David Tennant's character Hector says. People seriously overestimated the strength of Germany, especially its air force. But the majority did genuinely believe that Germany had an enormous power to flatten us with carpet bombing and there was a real fear there. Except for Churchill and the anti-appeasers, everyone in power and a large proportion of the population felt that if we went to war we would probably lose. It wasn't totally logical but it was that belief that fuelled the popular support for appeasement, along with the very understandable desire not to go to war so recently after the last war. After the incredible tragedy of the First World War, of course most people were reluctant to go to war again, after they had lost their sons, husbands and fathers. But one of the terrible ironies was that so many people's lives could have been saved if they had called Hitler's bluff.

MD   And this is what Hector puts into words so eloquently at the party. Could we talk about Hector as a representative of this small group of about thirty MPs who were against appeasement?

SP   The reason why the Secret Service and Chamberlain and the people around him were able to monitor the people opposing appeasement quite so thoroughly is because they were a very small bunch. The Tories had a huge majority in Parliament and any meaningful opposition could only come from within their party, but there were some influential people who were incredibly opposed to appeasement. One was Churchill; another was Anthony Eden, but he was, as proved when he was Prime Minister, rather an insubstantial figure, lacking bravery and finding it very difficult to fight any cause. Harold Macmillan, another future Prime Minister, was so passionately against appeasement that he shocked people. In his local cinema he stood up when he saw Chamberlain on the screen and started yelling at the cinema screen and waving an imaginary umbrella. That's not something you associate with British politicians, screaming at a cinema screen, let alone Harold Macmillan. There were one or two other older characters such as Leo Amery, who made the famous speech directed at Chamberlain quoting Cromwell: 'You've sat too long here for any good you've been doing. Depart, I say, and let us have done with you. In the name of God, go.' So it was a small bunch of committed people who saw the madness of trying to do a deal with Hitler. It has to be said that all the people around Chamberlain – including the newspaper editors – were in a very convenient denial about Hitler because it suited them so well to believe that he wasn't quite so dangerous.

MD   There are some wonderful glimpses in the film of life going on as normal. One of these is the party that Aunt Elizabeth boasts about having stayed up all night for. When Gilbert and Anne enter the house, they take a glimpse into a room filled with beautiful young women who are sleeping off the effects of the all-night-long party.

SP   I wanted very much to indicate the great parties of 1939, so *Glorious 39* has a triple meaning: it's not just the weather, which people remember as being particularly beautiful just before war was declared, but Anne's nickname is Glorious, and for the aristocracy it was a particularly glorious summer, not just with the wonderful parties in London, which I've alluded to, but the ball in Blenheim Palace in the summer of 1939, which the diarist Channon writes about memorably. It was one of the greatest balls of the twentieth century and was, within a few weeks of war, immensely extravagant even though people knew they were on the edge of a precipice. But we'd been on the edge of a precipice the year before and war had been averted, so people thought it would not happen. So it's a very well-documented time. And one of the extraordinary facts about the eve of war was that there was a move by the anti-appeasers to stop Parliament rising for their usual long holiday and Chamberlain made this scornful speech deriding the idea that they should give up their holiday. And we're talking within six weeks of the war being declared, and remember that, in March, Hitler had broken the Munich agreement and marched into the rest of Czechoslovakia. So even after that and after trenches being dug in Hyde Park, the idea that they should give up their holiday and stay in crisis seemed to them comical and was ridiculed in Parliament. And there was a massive majority that voted to go off on holiday so they then all had to come rushing back again.

MD   And do you think that you were distilling a range of disbelief and anger when you were selecting details to put into the film?

SP   Well, surprise is a good creative urge and you want the rest of the world to be as surprised as you are. And because I'm making a suspenseful story I've bottled the essence of this background and let it seep into the film so you get the family with the trappings of this aristocratic life, the country house, the aftermath of a great ball and the shock of them having to come back from the country house. I'm fuelled by wonder at what a close run it was, that we stood up to Hitler in the end, and I just wanted to explore how to dramatise that for a modern audience in an enjoyable way; I hope to enthral them as I'm enthralled by that period and I thought this was a good way of doing it.

MD   You've chosen to locate the drama within a family and it's reminiscent of your other work in that respect. It's a film about a family, about secrets gradually unravelling as one member of that family goes on a journey of discovery. Can you tell me about your choice of Anne as the protagonist?

SP   The reason for it being seen through Anne's eyes is because it's easier to distil things through a small group of characters that you get to know well. And appeasement was a passionate dividing line in families but, also, there were within families a lot of people who were like Anne who didn't take a huge interest in foreign affairs, as is still true. There was very little reported about what was really going on in Germany, and so the British people – unless they were part of the Foreign Office like Ralph or the political class – would not be aware that when the Anschluss happened, for instance, Jewish families were made to scrub the streets, deprived of their livelihoods and their status and prevented from leaving Vienna and hauled off trains. In Anne's case, she is apolitical at the beginning of the story, although a natural rebel in the sense that she has a lover at home, she's an actress, she's not a conventional deb, and she is someone who leads her own independent life, which was still unusual for women at that time. And why did I make her adopted? It's obviously important that what happens to Anne has a wider resonance and, as we know in Europe, if you were not of the right bloodstock you were extremely vulnerable once the Third Reich had control. Through that combination of being adopted and being an actress, Anne doesn't have many people to defend her, she hasn't got a husband or a family, and she is vulnerable in that sense. I wanted to show that the Bill Nighy character is culpable in a very human way. He's not Satan; I didn't want him to be someone who's revealed as a Nazi. I wanted to show that he loves his adopted daughter, but he loves his life, his real children and his country, as he sees it, more.

MD   Towards the end of the film he refers to all the things that he loves: the values of civilisation, democracy and art. These are all threatened by war, and it's his justification for appeasement in his speech to Anne.

SP   A lot of people believed that there was no alternative, that we would be destroyed. It was sort of self-fulfilling; they didn't take huge steps to find out whether this was true or not. Also, many men who survived the First World War were scarred by that experience, it was the most extraordinary, hellish, unimaginable horror, and of course they didn't want that happening again. The character played by Bill [Nighy] was in the trenches and, of course, had seen the horror and was haunted by it. He also wants the life he so values to continue and is prepared to do a great deal to make sure that it is not interfered with. The language of people who disagreed with the supporters of Churchill was very intemperate and there are many quotes of them saying that those who opposed appeasing Hitler should be shot or tried for treason and that, if there's a war, it's all the fault of the Jews. I've left that out of Alexander's makeup; I didn't want him to go into a violently anti-Semitic speech, although his treatment of Anne is sufficient to show a distinction between people that are born with the 'right' blood and those that aren't.

MD   We talked about the war and the threat of war splitting families. At the start of the film it's Anne who seems the strongest of the three siblings and it's only later in the film that we realise there might have been a division between the siblings right from the beginning. Is this something you wanted to convey?

SP   I think sibling rivalry happens in most families and sometimes you're unaware of it until quite late in life. And the siblings here are all very close in age, and Anne was the first one, even though she's adopted, and because she's got quite a strong character it's natural for her to take charge of arrangements. This is especially true because the mum is a bit checked out of things, which is also I think quite an accurate reflection of certain forms of English upper-class life at the time. I also didn't want the mum to be a sophisticated character like Aunt Elizabeth, because then they would have become a completely satanic family and I wanted it to be truthful. The scene when the mum lets Anne out of the room at the end to me is the most suggestive of what life would have been like in Britain if we had capitulated to Hitler, what happened all over Europe in fact, when people would suddenly be staring down as their neighbours were being made to lick the pavement as people goose-stepped around them, yelled at them and beat them. So the fact of Anne being unaware of the sibling rivalry is like those neighbours; suddenly it erupts into something ghastly.

MD   I wonder if we could consider a particular episode of the film to chart the development of Anne's realisation of what's going on. One of the early scenes illustrating a symbolic transgression is the crossing of the shell line and going into the shed where she discovers the foxtrot records. Could you talk about your decision to use that as a precipitator of the following plot?

SP   I wanted the discovery to be at home but not to implicate the family. I also wanted the feeling that, in pure storytelling terms, the whole family is somehow doomed, so it's a surprise when all are implicated. And you feel that Alexander isn't with Balcombe until much later. I also liked the idea of there being an area where the children weren't allowed to go because there was this great abbey so close and they could use that as a place to play instead and to make up stories. Norfolk is full of these ruins, it's quite sparsely populated, it's always been a bit Establishment in its sympathies and it's full of quite private houses, often with links to the Royal Family. Little Walsingham, where this was filmed, is a famous place of pilgrimage because of the abbey, and so those things were an interesting cocktail, with the real history of Norfolk seeping into the film.

MD   You've very successfully created a sense of centuries-old tradition in centring the drama in this family. There's a sense of continuity that is now being threatened. Another scene that shows how Anne might be being played with by the rest of the family is the picnic on the family estate when Anne's left to look after the baby. Can you talk about the significance of this scene?

SP   From a dramatic point of view, the story needed to create suspense, and the sense of Anne's authority being chipped away. The main engine of that is this incident at the picnic and what I tried to do is show that the situation isn't totally black and white. Anne did have an erotic reverie thinking of her lover and so she was a tiny bit culpable, but she didn't in any way endanger the baby's safety by just dozing off. But Balcombe sees this opportunity and gets the child to move the baby, so that if Anne wakes she doesn't see Balcombe with the baby. So it's a clever thing to do and it works as a moment of complete panic on her part and it plays to her vulnerabilities. Because she's an actress, her authority is pulled from under her and that was the point of doing it, because Balcombe casts her as an absent-minded, unreliable actress. Later when she's in the car with Gilbert she says, 'I know you don't believe me after the incident with the baby and the pushchair,' and he says 'Oh no,' but you still think he has reservations. So even with her friend it does undermine her authority, and that appalling sense of being left in charge and doing something wrong also works as a good piece of suspense.

MD   I think it's the first time we've identified Anne as an outsider within the family. Later, in what for me is the most horrifying scene in the whole film, we see her as an outsider much more vividly when she chooses to meet Lawrence at the vet's. It's the most horrifying and troubling episode in the whole film because of both what happens then and what her father does to secure her or to shut her up.

SP   I've already talked about the historical basis for the pets being put down and I thought the fact that they were being slaughtered in these numbers and piled up in the streets was an effortless metaphor for what might have happened to all the other undesirables, the gypsies, Jews, homosexuals, trade unionists, leftists, Communists, everybody they didn't like. I also wanted the sense of the way bureaucracy takes over and can be so easily used for evil. I show that with the policeman taunting Anne when *habeas corpus* is abolished, and then with the rather nice lady at the vet's. I wanted to show how easy it was for a vet, who was used to curing animals, to put them down on an industrial scale. This was an extraordinarily important image for the story, to hint at what might have been.

MD   You've written an incredible part for Romola Garai, who plays Anne. Did you write that part, or indeed any other parts, with particular actors in mind?

SP   No, I didn't write it with Romola in mind, but I knew it was such a demanding and large part that there were only a few people in Britain who were up to it. I had watched Romola's career with great interest since she debuted in cinema in *I Capture the Castle*, which I thought she was lovely in, and then more recently she was sensational in *Atonement*. And she's an extra-ordinary actress and enormously intelligent and articulate, but she also commits all the time. She asks lots of questions, which I really like and it's very much a dialogue with her. We did a great deal of rehearsal with all the actors, but especially with Romola. I always rehearse a lot and it's because I think that when you have these big journeys for my characters, you can't just turn up on the day of filming and do it, people have to feel secure. There's no time-pressure in rehearsal, there's a chance to talk about the history which you can't really do on the set, so it's very useful. I did have Bill Nighy in mind when I wrote it. He's always been the nice guy in the other two shows I've done with him, *The Lost Prince* and *Gideon's Daughter*; in this he's a much darker creation and I thought that was a very inter-esting journey for us because that's something we hadn't done together. Nobody else I had in mind, although it's fabulous to have Julie Christie playing Aunt Elizabeth. She's quite a pin-up of my youth; she was one of the biggest stars in the world when I was at school. And there are two other great figures from my youth: Christopher Lee, such an iconic figure of British cinema, and Jenny Agutter. Again, Jenny was a great figure of my youth, from *Walkabout* and *The Railway Children* and those British movies. So we had those legends of the British cinema, plus this great swirl of young talent. For Hector, I needed somebody really vivid because, although he's only on screen for ten minutes or so, he dominates the action for a long time, so he needs to make a real impression and you need to miss him. For this reason, David Tennant is the perfect choice. Hugh Bonneville as Gilbert has something very touching about him but melancholic as well, which makes you think maybe he did shoot himself because he was rather unhappy with his career and there's a sense of an unfulfilled life. So, it was a great company of actors; I was incredibly lucky to have them in freezing Norfolk.

MD   You write your screenplays very deliberately, so as a reader you can picture it exactly. And you directed so you can ensure the fulfilment of your vision but, nevertheless, with this stellar range of actors, were there any surprises?

SP   There are always surprises with actors; they always bring something that you hadn't foreseen. The main surprises were from Romola because I hadn't worked with her before. Romola is in every scene and she's a very strong character and, although we worked everything out in rehearsal, there was an extra dimension when we were filming. For instance, in the scene between Anne and Balcombe when she's in bed at the end and he's sitting there, for the first half of the scene she wasn't looking at him at all and I was expecting her to stare at him, to try to work out if he's lying or not. But when I saw what Romola was doing I thought it was a brilliant choice – not even wanting to contemplate what he's telling her until she really has to look at him. So those sorts of things, small but enormous when you see it put together, make a big difference. I love working with actors and I hope I'm good with actors because I respect their intelligence. I'm a great believer in actors' intelligence and their instincts and, although sometimes they need to be challenged and guided in a different direction and I'm not afraid to do that, it's always a partnership.

GLORIOUS 39

Glorious 39 was produced by BBC Films, the UK Film Council, Screen East Content Investment Fund and Quickfire Films for Talkback Thames in association with Magic Light Pictures, and was released in November 2009. The cast was as follows:

Anne	Romola Garai
Alexander	Bill Nighy
Aunt Elizabeth	Julie Christie
Ralph	Eddie Redmayne
Celia	Juno Temple
Maud	Jenny Agutter
Gilbert	Hugh Bonneville
Lawrence	Charlie Cox
Oliver	Corin Redgrave
Hector	David Tennant
Balcombe	Jeremy Northam
Walter	Christopher Lee
Michael	Toby Regbo
Vicar	Nicholas Blane
Lucy	Katharine Burford
Mick	Asier Newman
Kathleen	Jane Fowler
Young Walter	Sam Kubrick-Finney
Betty	Angela Terence
Director	Tom Goodman-Hill
Military Policeman	Anthony Flanagan
Miss Crowley	Suzanne Burden
Vet	Richard Cordery
Mrs Knight	Joy McBrinn
Old Anne	Muriel Pavlow
Michael's Mother	Sharon Bower
Solider Guarding Door	Ryan Kiggell

Writer/Director Stephen Poliakoff
Producers Barney Reisz and Martin Pope
Director of Photography Danny Cohen
Music Adrian Johnston
Editor Jason Krasucki
Production Designer Mark Leese
Hair and Make-Up Designer Jenny Shircore
Costume Designer Annie Symons
Casting Director Andy Pryor
Line Producer Julie Clark

EXT. NORFOLK LANDSCAPES AND RUINED ABBEY. 1939. DAY.
A very wide shot of the Norfolk countryside, fields stretching out towards the horizon, the sky dwarfing the three figures running towards us. These are the siblings, ANNE, RALPH *and* CELIA; *they are at first tiny dots on the horizon and we just hear their laughter and voices echoing towards us. They are dressed in the clothes of the late thirties.*

ANNE, *the oldest, is leading the way. She is a vibrant young woman in her mid-twenties, confident, the one with the most natural authority, as if she is used to making the decisions for the other two, but she also has a rebellious, anarchic smile.*

RALPH *is very close to her in age. He has sharp, humorous eyes suggesting somebody who looks at the world as an amused observer.*

CELIA, *who is about twenty, is bringing up the rear. She has a dreamy, abstracted air, a delicate porcelain quality.*

As they near us we cut behind them and track rapidly with them. A sense of exuberant exploration as they move across the ridge in the field. Below them stretched out across a gentle valley are the ruins of a large abbey surrounded by trees. A medieval gatehouse is almost perfectly preserved; behind it are jagged ruins, the pillars of the abbey left jutting towards the open sky.

The siblings move towards the abbey. There is the distant sound of a foxtrot playing, at first hardly audible.

They move through the maze of the pillars as if they are very used to coming to this place. But the music is getting louder, and is clearly an unfamiliar sound in the ruins they know well.

They begin to slow; the camera slows with them, curling round the last pillar.

In the distance in the shadows of the medieval gatehouse are four men in dark city suits and wearing hats. There is a wind-up gramophone on a small table playing the music.

The three siblings watch from a distance, keeping out of sight.
There is something very disconcerting about the men. They
are moving slowly, deliberately, they have been digging, and
the siblings can see the earth has been disturbed and a shallow
ditch dug.

In the shadows behind the men there is a strange shape lying
on the ground, swathed in a sheet and tied with rope. The
siblings can't quite make out whether it is a human body or
some other unidentifiable bundle. In the deep shadows behind
the men are more sacks.

The image gradually moves into slow motion, the men digging
and talking, the foxtrot getting louder and louder. The men
slowly look up and look straight at the siblings and the camera.
The siblings instantly retreat into the shadows, uncertain if they
have been seen. We return to the men staring at the camera.
CELIA *and* RALPH *move off as if to get a closer look.* ANNE
follows them. The shot moves around a pillar and fades to
black.

EXT. MODERN CITY LANDSCAPE / ST PAUL'S. DAY.
THE PRESENT.
Abrupt cut to modern London, the landscape around St Paul's,
a jumble of cranes, large modern buildings crowding near the
cathedral, the river stretching close.

We dissolve through shots of this landscape until we pick out
a boy of seventeen, MICHAEL, *walking through the maze of*
little streets, the fragment that survives of the medieval street
plan around Carter Lane.

MICHAEL *is a young man of studious appearance, he is*
wearing a suit as if he has made himself specially smart for this
occasion. In one hand he is holding a bulky file, in the other a
street map which he turns and twists as he finds himself
increasingly lost in the labyrinth of little streets.

Once we are down on street level with him, we find ourselves in a world of dark alleyways suddenly opening out into hidden squares with ancient names like the King's Wardrobe.

All the time we are conscious of the cathedral being very close; we see low angle shots of its dome towering over the whole district, and we can hear its bells.

MICHAEL *stops, very lost now. A cat is watching him from behind some railings. Their eyes meet.* MICHAEL *turns and retraces his steps and suddenly realises he has walked straight past the entrance of another dark alleyway.*

He goes into the alleyway and finds himself in a cul-de-sac dominated by a large eighteenth-century house. The house has all its windows shuttered and looks uninhabited, but this is the place he has been looking for.

He moves up to the front door and rings the bell.

An old man's voice rasps out of the entrance phone, which hisses and crackles.

RASPING VOICE: Yes?

MICHAEL: Hello . . . ? (*Nervously.*) It's Michael here . . .
　　Michael Walton. Is Mr Page there . . . ?
　　There is a loud crackle.

RASPING VOICE: Which one do you want?

MICHAEL (*hesitates*): Both if possible . . .
　　There is a pause. For a moment we stay on MICHAEL*'s nervous face. Then the entry lock is released with a loud piercing buzz.*

INT. THE OLD HOUSE. STAIRCASE. DAY.
Inside the house MICHAEL *stares up the steep staircase. The interior is exceptionally dark and looks like it hasn't been redecorated for many years.*

All the way up the stairs are piles of second-hand books. The rasping voice is calling out to him.

RASPING VOICE: Come on up, Michael . . .

> MICHAEL *climbs up the old staircase, holding tight on to his file.*

INT. THE OLD HOUSE. MAIN RECEPTION ROOM. DAY.
MICHAEL *enters a wood-panelled room which has no daylight in it at all. The window is firmly shuttered and the room is lit by table lamps.*

> *Two old men are sitting in the semi-darkness:* WALTER, *the one with the rasping voice, and* OLIVER. *They are both dressed in dark suits, white shirts and maroon ties.*

On a table in front of them tea is already laid out, a fine china teapot and a cherry cake.

> *The room is cluttered with books, papers and black-and-white framed photographs. It is seemingly a total time warp, almost unchanged since the war, although there is a fairly modern computer in the corner.*

> *The two old men stare at* MICHAEL *beadily out of the shadows.*

WALTER: I am Walter . . . and this is Oliver.

> OLIVER *gives* MICHAEL *a faint smile.*

And you are our cousin Michael . . .

MICHAEL: Yes . . . (*He stares back nervously.*) That's me . . .

WALTER: I believe we met once when you were six months old.

OLIVER: I am sure he remembers it vividly!

> *They both stare at* MICHAEL.

WALTER: Have some cake . . .

EXT. ST PAUL'S. DAY.
We cut to a low angle shot of St Paul's, its brooding presence dwarfing the surrounding buildings despite the modern office blocks clustering round it. The bells begin to chime for evensong.

INT. THE WOOD-PANELLED ROOM. DAY.
We cut back to MICHAEL *in the middle of a mouthful of cherry
cake. The evensong bells are really loud, almost making the
room shake.*

    MICHAEL *wipes the crumbs off his lips.*

MICHAEL: Delicious cake . . .
    The old men are staring at him.
        MICHAEL *glances round the strange room. He sees a
    framed photograph on the wall of St Paul's, an iconic
    image of the cathedral during the blitz. Next to it is a
    child's drawing of a knight in armour, and next to that is
    a photograph of* WALTER *and* OLIVER *as children.*
    OLIVER *is a toddler in a pushchair.*
MICHAEL: Is that the two of you?
OLIVER: It is indeed . . . as I am sure you've guessed, I am
    the baby!
    *Lurking beneath the pictures are two very old radios, and
    in the corner there is a third.*
MICHAEL: You do have a lot of radios . . .
WALTER: We do, yes.
OLIVER: They are from our childhood . . . You want to
    hear one?
    OLIVER *leans over and clicks a switch on one of the old
    sets. No sound comes out.* OLIVER*'s beady eyes looking at*
    MICHAEL.
    It will take a moment to warm up . . .
WALTER: What do you want to ask both of us, Michael?
MICHAEL: Right, yes!
    *He grabs his file and pulls out a family album, putting it
    down in front of him. He starts turning the pages fast. We
    see it is full of family photographs, cuttings from newspapers,
    old postcards, all carefully labelled and stuck to the page.*
    I've just got one question really . . . I am very

interested in history – family history in particular –
and you are the only ones left from that time.

WALTER: Yes?

*MICHAEL stops at a photograph in the album. We see it
is of* CELIA, *the youngest of the siblings.* MICHAEL *stares
at her.*

MICHAEL: My grandmother, of course.

He turns the page.

I just wondered . . .

He stops again by a picture of ANNE, *seemingly a still from
a play. She is kneeling on the floor looking up at someone.*

What happened to her sister?

He points at the photo of ANNE.

To her?

He looks up. Both men are staring at him, very surprised.

MICHAEL: Do you know?

WALTER (*quietly*): She was an actress . . .

OLIVER: She was! She made some films . . . ! She played
the best friend or the schoolteacher, those sort of
parts.

WALTER: There she is . . . up there – (*Pointing at a
photograph.*) With your grandmother and her brother
Ralph.

Deep in the shadows MICHAEL *can just make out the
photograph* WALTER *is pointing at. It is of the three
siblings leaning on a gate in a field, laughing together.*

MICHAEL: Oh yes . . . there she is!

*Out of the corner of his eye he can see the old radio has
started to light up; it is now glowing with a pale orange
light and sounds begin to crackle out of it.*

WALTER: Anne was the oldest . . . She was adopted, of
course. As frequently seems to happen, they were
desperate for children, didn't think they could have
any – and so they adopted one – and then lo and
behold along come the babies anyway! (*He glances at*

the picture of the siblings.) They were all very close . . .
OLIVER *is moving the dial on the radio, modern sounds,
little bursts of talking, different languages coming out of
the old set.*

OLIVER: You like the wireless? You didn't think it would
work, did you?! (*He moves the dial.*) Let's see if we can
find something more appropriate . . .

MICHAEL: What happened to her?

WALTER *stares straight into* MICHAEL*'s eyes. There is
something distinctly frightening about the old man.*
MICHAEL *swallows.*

MICHAEL: Tell me . . .

WALTER: It's not always a good place to go, Michael, the
past . . .

MICHAEL: *Please.*

*Out of the wireless suddenly comes some nostalgic music,
the sound faint and crackly.*

OLIVER: This is a little bit better . . . Let's see if we can get
a clearer signal . . .

*We are very close on the radio, on the bright orange glow,
and as the dial begins to move again, we cut to the past.*

EXT. NORFOLK COUNTRYSIDE AND HOUSE. 1939.
AFTERNOON.
*An intense lush landscape in north Norfolk: rolling fields and
large skies, strong late-afternoon light. The images are voluptuously
beautiful, a totally unspoilt corner of the world. We see a fine
eighteenth-century house nestling in a small valley, surrounded
by medieval walls surviving from an earlier building. Within the
medieval walls lies an elaborate garden with views across the
valley and a cluster of outbuildings.*

*The camera begins to move through the garden towards the
house. We hear* WALTER*'s rasping voice continuing over the
images.*

WALTER (*voice-over*): It had been a fantastic summer, that
    summer of '39, the most glorious summer most
    people could remember for a very long time.

    A year before it had seemed war with Germany had
    been averted, the policy of appeasing Hitler, of
    reasoning with him, really had worked . . . and even
    now it seemed it might still work . . .
    *The camera is getting closer to the house. On the terrace of
    the house we see a long table covered in candles and
    decorations. It is set for a celebratory meal. The candles are
    not lit yet. The camera is moving all the time.*
    Your grandmother, and Anne and Ralph, had grown
    up in the most beautiful house . . . with an even more
    beautiful garden.
    We are getting close to the table. We see ANNE *and* RALPH
    and CELIA *putting the last decorations into place.*
    It was a very exciting time . . . Ralph was doing
    well at the Foreign Office, Anne had a part she was
    excited about in a new movie . . . it was your great-
    grandfather's birthday, and they had prepared the
    most wonderful table for him – or rather Anne had,
    because she was in charge of most things . . .
    *The sound of the past comes rushing towards us as the
    camera reaches the table. We hear a gramophone playing
    a dance from somewhere in the house. We are close on the
    table decorations, a line of flags marching along the table;
    on them has been painted a series of fat, red-faced knights
    battling, riding and dancing.*

CELIA (*smiling a radiant smile*): It's perfect . . . Papa will
    love it!

RALPH (*flicking one of the flags*): The Fat Men on the
    march . . . ! (*To* ANNE.) It's one of your very best
    tables . . .

We hear laughter from the garden. In the shadow of the
trees are two young men who are talking animatedly:
LAWRENCE, *a very handsome man in his twenties, and*
HECTOR, *who is slightly older.* HECTOR *has a slightly*
manic appearance, talking very fast and waving his arms
around.

HECTOR: Have you heard about Chamberlain and musical
chairs?

LAWRENCE: Musical chairs? No, I haven't.

HECTOR: He loves playing musical chairs, he goes down to
Cliveden to stay with the Astors and they say, 'Oh,
let's play musical chairs,' because they know the
Prime Minister is so keen on it and they let him win
every time. And he never notices anything is wrong!
That it's been fixed. That's the kind of man he is.

LAWRENCE: Is he stupid then? Because you'd have to be
really stupid not to notice.

HECTOR: No, he's vain, vain beyond belief, and that makes
him stupid!

We cut back to ANNE *and* CELIA *watching them.*

CELIA (*indicating* LAWRENCE): I like your new friend.

HECTOR *gesticulating as he talks.*

The other one's a little dotty, isn't he?!

ANNE: Maybe a little . . . but he can be great fun.

CELIA (*softly, watching* LAWRENCE): Anne, he is beautiful.
I think he is the most gorgeous man I have ever seen.

ANNE (*laughs*): That's why he's here!

ANNE *swaps a couple of the knights around on the table.*
Suddenly LAWRENCE *is by her side, staring down at the*
decorations on the table.

LAWRENCE (*his tone soft, intimate*): Why all the knights?
What are they up to?

ANNE: Ah . . . it's something we started as children . . .

RALPH: They're absolutely everywhere! Want to see?

INT. THE HOUSE. FIRST-FLOOR LANDING. LATE
AFTERNOON.
They are upstairs in the house: ANNE, CELIA, RALPH,
LAWRENCE *and* HECTOR. CELIA *pushes open the door of*
ANNE's *bedroom.*

CELIA: We can show them your room, can't we, Anne?
     Because that's where the best ones are . . . !
     As the siblings show LAWRENCE *and* HECTOR *the*
     knights, the following sequences melt into each other, with
     LAWRENCE *and* ANNE *always physically very close.*
         LAWRENCE *peers into* ANNE's *bedroom. There is a*
     whole series of drawings of the portly knights pinned up
     along one of the walls like a frieze. The drawings are comic,
     but also full of detail. Below the drawings a grumpy-
     looking cat is sitting on the bed.
ANNE: I must point out I did these when I was much
     younger!
RALPH: It's all her fault! She started it, and then we all did
     them . . . We call them 'Fat Men Dancing'.
ANNE: And now there is no escaping them!
LAWRENCE (*staring at the cat*): And he looks like he might
     be about to start doing them too . . .
ANNE: That's George . . . his sister Sonia disappeared a
     few days ago, so he is a little upset . . . We've got to
     find her, haven't we, George?
     ANNE *and* LAWRENCE's *fingers touch.*

EXT. THE GARDEN AND OUTBUILDINGS. LATE AFTERNOON.
We cut to another image of the fat knights painted on a garden
wall, and then we see smaller knights on flowerpots and even on
the railings.
     The siblings, LAWRENCE *and* HECTOR *are now moving*
through the garden near the outbuildings.

HECTOR (*staring at the knights, smiling*): I'm sure they're all
    historically accurate! Were you allowed to put them
    absolutely everywhere you wanted? Nobody said no?
RALPH: Almost everywhere! (*Indicating the outbuildings.*)
    We were not allowed in those.
CELIA: This is the shell line . . .
    She indicates a line of sea shells stretching across the
    gravel at the entrance to the outbuildings. A subtle but
    clear barrier.
    We were not allowed to cross it.
ANNE: Because those buildings were stuffed with all Papa's
    papers that he uses for his books.
    LAWRENCE *stops at the edge of the shell line.*
LAWRENCE: I bet you did cross it though – you must have?
RALPH: No! Never have! We didn't need to – there were so
    many other places to play . . . (*He suddenly turns.*)
    Want to see where it all started?
CELIA: We have time to go, don't we, Anne? Papa's not
    back till seven . . . and we are so well prepared. Let's
    take them there, Anne! Please! (*She looks at her elder*
    sister.) Say yes!
ANNE: Yes.
    CELIA *smiles delightedly.*
    If we are quick . . .

EXT. THE ABBEY RUINS. LATE AFTERNOON.
We cut to them moving through the ruins of the abbey. HECTOR
is calling, making a loud booming noise to test the echo.
LAWRENCE *and* ANNE *together, standing very close, watching*
him.

HECTOR: Marvellous place to come to rehearse one's
    speeches! I must start using it immediately!
RALPH: Anne spends all her time here learning her lines . . .

RALPH *leaps boyishly on to one of the low walls.*

RALPH: This is where it all comes from – the stories we made up – about chubby men doing heroic things!

ANNE: They were always deeply flawed, our knights – overweight and lazy . . .

CELIA: We like them like that!

ANNE: But they were quite brave when we wanted them to be. (*She mimes a sword battle.*) They slaughtered everybody that dared attack them!

HECTOR (*letting out another bellow*): Your father used to make terrific speeches in the House of Commons – in fact I've copied him once or twice. It's a pity he speaks so less often now.

ANNE: Well, his health has always been delicate, so that's why he's taking more of a back seat now.

LAWRENCE: I've heard a lot about your papa – that he is the most charming man in England. (*He smiles.*) And that makes me very nervous – what if he doesn't like me?

ANNE (*lightly, softly*): I think he probably will . . .

INT./EXT. THE TERRACE AND GROUND-FLOOR RECEPTION ROOM. EARLY EVENING.

It is evening now, the sun just setting. The candles are all lit. We see in the distance coming towards us across the reception room ALEXANDER, *the siblings' father. He is a handsome man in his fifties. He has a youthful smile and a charming, relaxed manner. For a politician his appearance is unconventional: his hair slightly longer than normal, his tone informal, he looks more like an artist or a poet. A maid,* LUCY, *is fluttering around him, seeing if he needs anything, as if she is used to his delicate constitution.*

Behind him are two official-looking men, BALCOMBE *and another thin-faced man,* APPLEBY. BALCOMBE *is a tall man*

with a handsome face and sharp, glinty eyes. All the men are
still wearing their coats.
    We cut to ALEXANDER*'s point of view and see the siblings*
standing waiting, with ANNE *at the front. A powerful tracking*
shot towards them, with the candles flickering on the table.

ALEXANDER: What a glorious homecoming!
    He reaches the terrace and stares down at the beautiful
    table decorations.
    Anne, you have surpassed yourself – absolutely
    surpassed yourself! You all have. (*He indicates*
    APPLEBY.) Henry you've met, of course, and this is
    Joseph Balcombe, a colleague of Henry's . . . Joseph,
    these are my children.
BALCOMBE (*greeting the siblings*): It is a delightful surprise
    to find it is your father's birthday.
ALEXANDER (*studies the table settings*): Need I ask – your
    mother is still getting ready?
CELIA: Naturally! (*Indicating the floral display.*) But she did
    all the flowers, of course!
    HECTOR *and* LAWRENCE *are waiting on the other side*
    of the table; we can see LAWRENCE *is distinctly nervous.*
    ALEXANDER *greets* HECTOR *with a familiar tone.*
ALEXANDER: Hector, very good to see you here!
    He turns his attention to LAWRENCE, *studies him for a*
    moment.
    And you must be Lawrence . . .
LAWRENCE: I am. (*Trying to sound relaxed.*) How do you
    do, sir. And happy birthday!
ALEXANDER: Well, you certainly live up to Anne's
    description of you.
ANNE (*smiles*): Papa!
LAWRENCE (*embarrassed laugh*): There is no easy reply to
    that . . .
RALPH (*to* ANNE, *grinning*): What did you say? Did you say

he is one of the cleverest people in the Foreign Office
and I had better watch out! Because that's the truth.

EXT. THE TERRACE. EVENING.
*It is now dusk. They are all sitting at the long table on the
terrace eating their first course. The men are in dinner jackets.*
ALEXANDER *is sitting at the centre of the table, the siblings all
close to him. And next to him is his wife,* MAUD, *a very quiet,
contained woman who seems a little remote, as if she occupies
a world of her own.*

At the end of the table is HECTOR *and at the opposite end is*
BALCOMBE, *a powerful silent presence, eating slowly.*

MAUD: Why are you here in these parts, Mr Balcombe?
BALCOMBE: A little fishing, I'm very partial to a little
    fishing. It's been such a perfect summer, which
    annoyingly I have had to miss through work, but
    I was absolutely determined to get in some fishing
    somehow.
MAUD: How very sensible.
BALCOMBE: And coming here, to such an ancient place . . .
    it's quite possible to think all is right with the world.
HECTOR (*suddenly erupting at the end of the table*): But it
    isn't, is it!
    They all look up.
    We are not even sleepwalking any more towards
    disaster, are we?! We are actually going up to it and
    welcoming it with open arms!
ALEXANDER (*smiling at* HECTOR *indulgently*): Well, I've
    certainly been known to do that in my time . . . !
BALCOMBE: Precisely in what way are we doing that?
HECTOR: Precisely in what way?! I will tell you absolutely
    precisely – we're not content with letting Hitler march
    into Czechoslovakia and Austria, now we're saying

that's absolutely all right old chap – take some more
countries if you really want, if you suddenly feel the
need, take some more!

ANNE *watches* HECTOR, *with his arms gesticulating wildly
all over the place. Her eyes meet* LAWRENCE's *who is
sitting across from her. Their strong mutual attraction is
obvious. She looks away for a second, but then finds herself
looking straight back at him.* BALCOMBE *sips his wine.*

BALCOMBE: Are we saying that?

HECTOR: Yes, we are. Hitler is intent on taking over the
whole of Europe and we are letting him do it as long
as he doesn't bother us. That can't be allowed to go
on. Forgive a statement of the blindingly obvious –
or what *I* think is obvious – but evil has to be stood
up to . . .

BALCOMBE (*carefully rearranging his napkin*): Yes, but of
course one has to be in a position to do that – one has
to have the means.

HECTOR (*his hands flapping*): Of course we've got the
bloody means! Even if we have let Germany rearm,
we mustn't *exaggerate* how strong she is! Under this
current government, under Mr Chamberlain, who I
might remind you is my own leader, so I don't say
this lightly, we are behaving as if we have to avoid war
at absolutely all costs – so every day we do something
that actually makes the situation worse!

BALCOMBE (*quietly*): You really think that is true . . . ?
What did you have in mind?

LAWRENCE *gives* ANNE *a look across the table. She smiles
back.*

HECTOR: Well, to give you just one example, I heard
rumours – I've yet to find out if they are true or not –
but I heard the most extraordinary rumour we are
trying to interest the Nazis in accepting a gigantic
secret loan which we will negotiate for them on the

international markets – so they might turn their armaments industry back to peaceful means . . . We are actually planning to give them *money*!

ALEXANDER: Well, that does sound truly bizarre, Hector.

HECTOR: Alexander here fought in the war of course and got wounded, so I don't criticise him, but not enough other people are speaking out! – So it is clear it is up to young MPs like me to get rid of our present leadership, which is leading us straight towards our doom very quickly –

BALCOMBE: That is some claim, Mr Haldane, that we are heading for our doom . . .

HECTOR: Yes, and I am very aware it isn't a popular thing to say. The present leadership will stand no opposition, no criticism of any kind . . . (*He takes a mouthful of food, then suddenly continues.*) For instance, another thing I found out recently . . . the Secret Service are running this magazine *Truth* – a fairly hilarious title in the circumstances I think you'll agree – they're actually paying for this publication *Truth*, which people think of course is entirely independent . . . and in every issue they run a savage attack on anybody expressing views like mine, and of course on Winston Churchill in particular!

ANNE *and* LAWRENCE *are looking at each other.*

LAWRENCE *discreetly stretches his hand out across the table.* ANNE *feels her whole self being consumed with attraction.*

HECTOR: The Prime Minister, the present leadership, view Mr Churchill as dangerous because he would stand up to Hitler – he doesn't worry a bit about giving offence to the Nazis, he's not content to just mouth diplomatic banalities and wave his little umbrella like Mr Chamberlain!

BALCOMBE *sips his wine.*

So I feel I have to do everything in my power to make
sure Mr Churchill is not ignored . . . (*He munches.*)
And I believe I have a few things up my sleeve . . .
ANNE *touches* LAWRENCE'*s hand, their fingers entwine.*

EXT. THE FRONT OF THE HOUSE. NIGHT.
LAWRENCE *and* ANNE *are framed in the doorway of the house;
behind them is the drive.* BALCOMBE *and* APPLEBY *are getting
into a large car, a smaller two-seater is parked waiting for the
young men.* BALCOMBE *calls across at* ANNE *as he opens the
car door.*

BALCOMBE: A very pleasant evening, thank you.
    BALCOMBE *gets into the car.* ANNE *is very close to*
    LAWRENCE, *their bodies touch, she whispers to him.*
ANNE: Come on Thursday . . . the house will be empty in
    the afternoon.
    They can hardly stop touching each other. LAWRENCE
    gives her a kiss on the cheek, their lips hover close.
ANNE: Will you still be down here on Thursday? Can you
    come?
LAWRENCE: Yes, I'll still be at Cranmore, I can come . . .
    Their mouths very close.
    Suddenly HECTOR *appears behind them. He is staring
    at the front passenger seat of the car;* BALCOMBE'*s face is
    staring back at them through the windscreen, a powerful
    look.*
HECTOR: Who is that man?! (*His tone sounds worried,
    almost scared; he watches* BALCOMBE.) A strange,
    strange man . . .
    Suddenly we see a shot from BALCOMBE'*s point of view of*
    ANNE *standing with the two men,* HECTOR *whispering in
    her ear. We stay on* BALCOMBE *as the car moves off.*

INT. RECEPTION ROOM. NIGHT.
ALEXANDER *is sitting on a small settee in the reception room smoking a cigar. The room is entirely lit by candles. In the depth of field* CELIA *and* RALPH *are grouped around a gramophone, listening to some music.* MAUD *is putting garden flowers into a vase, arranging them carefully.* ANNE *sits on the settee next to her father.*

ALEXANDER: Thank you for such a wonderful birthday.
    He takes her hand.
ANNE: It wasn't spoilt by Hector?
ALEXANDER: No, I'm used to his fiery outbursts. (*He smiles.*) And of course there is always the possibility he could be right . . . (*He looks at her fondly.*) Will you read to me, darling? I love it when you read to me.
ANNE: What do you want me to read?
ALEXANDER: It doesn't matter . . . some Keats . . . anything.
    ANNE *reaches up to the bookshelf and takes down a book of poetry.* ALEXANDER *is watching* MAUD *arrange the flowers.*
    It's wonderful to have a passion, isn't it? Your mother's passion is her flowers, her garden – (*Looks at* ANNE.) and yours is your acting . . .
ANNE: And yours?
    The music playing, RALPH *and* CELIA *in the distance,* ALEXANDER *turns to* ANNE.
ALEXANDER (*softly*): My family . . .
    She begins to read Keats's 'Ode to Autumn' to her father.
    CELIA *takes the needle off the record,* RALPH *is still talking.*
CELIA: Sshhh . . . Anne's reading to Papa.

INT. ANNE'S BEDROOM. EARLY MORNING.
We track in on ANNE *as she lies in bed asleep. Dawn light.*
ANNE*'s eyes flicker. There is a sound, at first very faint, like a baby crying.*

Her eyes open; the sound is still there, but is now clearly the
sound of a cat, an urgent call. It sounds distressed.

ANNE *gets up and stares out of the window. She can't tell*
where the sound is coming from. She moves in her nightdress
and slippers on to the landing. The sound is a little louder,
coming somewhere from outside.

EXT. THE OUTBUILDINGS. EARLY MORNING.
ANNE *moves through the garden towards the outbuildings. The*
sound of the cat is growing much louder. She stops at the shell
line. She notices with interest it has been broken, disrupted.

She crosses it and moves towards the outbuilding where the
cat is crying. As she gets nearer she calls out.

ANNE: Sonia?

ANNE *presses her nose to the window of the shed. Inside*
she can see a very distressed cat crying out in the shadows.

ANNE: Sonia, really, how did you get in there?!

The cat stares at her.

We cut to ANNE *pulling open the large door of the*
second outbuilding, where a two-seater car is housed under
a very dusty tarpaulin. Above the car are a series of rusty
hooks. On one of the hooks is a bunch of keys.

We cut to ANNE *back by the door of the outbuilding the*
cat is trapped in.

She turns one key in the padlock and then another.
The second key works.

INT. THE OUTBUILDING. EARLY MORNING.
ANNE *moves inside the shed. She is greeted by piles of*
cardboard boxes and dark black files.

She begins to move towards Sonia, who is at the far end of
the shed.

ANNE: You've made me break the rules, Sonia . . .

She glances briefly at the boxes of papers.
What've you been doing, anyway . . . reading Papa's
manuscript about Napoleon?!
*She reaches the cat and is about to pick her up, when she
suddenly spots in among the boxes and files of paper the
incongruous sight of a row of about fifteen gramophone
records in brown paper sleeves.*

*She picks one of them up. It is labelled 'No, No, Nora:
Foxtrot'.*

*She looks at the label of another: 'Sweetheart We Need
Each Other'.*

ANNE (*laughs*): How did they get in here?
The cat watching her.
Been having a good listen, have you . . . ?!
She picks up another record: 'Some Sweet Day'.

*At that moment she hears a faint crunch on the gravel
outside. She looks up. She can see a shadow moving on the
ground through the open door of the shed. It's an extremely
fleeting glimpse; a second after she has seen it, it has gone.*
ANNE (*calls out*): Hello . . . ?
There is a silence.

ANNE *picks up a selection of three gramophone records
and the cat.*

EXT. THE GARDEN. EARLY MORNING.
ANNE *is moving back through the garden in the early-morning
light with the cat and the three gramophone records. She rounds
a corner and sees her mother, already fully dressed in gardening
clothes, quietly pruning.*
ANNE: Mama, you're up early.
MAUD (*smiles*): So much needs doing . . .
ANNE: I found Sonia!
MAUD: Yes. (*Concentrating on the pruning.*) That's splendid.

ANNE (*moves on, then stops*): You didn't see anybody pass
    by here, just now?
MAUD: No, my dear.
ANNE (*looks puzzled*): It must have been one of the servants.

INT. ANNE'S BEDROOM. EARLY MORNING.
ANNE *puts Sonia down on a chair in her bedroom.*

ANNE: We'll need to feed you up, won't we . . . ?
    ANNE *is staring with idle curiosity at the records, at the*
    title, 'Some Sweet Day'.
    Papa loves this one . . . !

INT./EXT. RECEPTION ROOM AND TERRACE. DAY.
ALEXANDER, RALPH *and* CELIA *are sitting at the long table on*
the terrace having breakfast. ANNE, *now dressed, moves towards*
them through the reception room carrying Sonia and one
gramophone record.

ANNE: Look who I've found! She got into one of the
    sheds.
RALPH (*laughs*): She obviously didn't realise it was
    forbidden territory. (*To Sonia.*) I thought you knew
    that!
ALEXANDER (*taking the cat*): The grumpy old girl, so good
    you're back.
ANNE: And look what I found there too – it was full of
    records . . . foxtrots . . . one of your favourites, Papa!
CELIA (*stroking Sonia*): She's been dancing in there too.
ALEXANDER: How odd . . . I don't think I ever put
    gramophone records in there. I wonder how that
    happened?

RALPH (*leaps up taking the record*): Let's see if it still plays.
We cut to the needle going on to the record on the
gramophone in the reception room.

    Instead of a foxtrot, we hear a recording of a crackling
telephone conversation, a harassed-sounding official, a
male voice.

MALE VOICE: Who is this? Who did you say you were?
We hear someone mumbling inaudibly at the other end.
I'm not sure why you are calling . . . Yes, I did receive
that . . . Yes, I believe I did . . .

RALPH (*grinning delightedly*): That's no foxtrot . . . I'd like
to see Papa dancing to that!

ALEXANDER (*staring at the gramophone, the voices mumbling*
on): That's very strange . . . I think this must be
Joseph's doing. (*He turns.*) Mr Balcombe asked if he
could store some government overflow with us . . .
they are drowning in paper, apparently.

ANNE (*laughing*): The government needs to store things
here?!

ALEXANDER: It seemed a harmless thing to do! The reason
he gave is interesting and quite funny – and rather
rude as well. He said there were very few places where
you could trust that servants won't go any more . . .
but knowing our servants that wasn't a worry here!

CELIA: He didn't say that did he? That *is* rude!

RALPH (*lightly*): He must mean they hardly manage to
clean the house, let alone the outbuildings!

CELIA: But people hadn't counted on Sonia and Anne!
Both CELIA *and* RALPH *are fizzing with excitement at the*
discovery.

ANNE: Why are they storing records which are labelled as
foxtrots?

RALPH: And which are clearly not! Probably their idea of
maximum security – 'Let's call everything after a

dance, that will fool everybody, nobody will ever see through that!'
He smiles joyfully and sends the records spinning through the air towards the trees.

ALEXANDER (*watching the records fly*): I know since Munich they have been recording a great number of government calls . . . because people's note-taking has been so inadequate. But I had no idea we had some here! (*He smiles.*) That's rather exciting . . .

INT. ANNE'S BEDROOM. AFTERNOON.
We cut to ANNE *and* LAWRENCE *kissing passionately in* ANNE*'s bedroom. Strong afternoon sun. There is a cat sitting on the bed.* LAWRENCE*'s shirt is unbuttoned,* ANNE *is in a slip.* ANNE *begins to pull* LAWRENCE*'s shirt off.*

LAWRENCE: Are you sure there's nobody here?
ANNE (*laughs*): There *shouldn't* be anybody here, not even the servants. They've all gone to the fête.
    She begins to unbutton his trousers.
LAWRENCE (*lightly*): Do we have to have George watching?
ANNE: That's Sonia . . .
LAWRENCE: Do we have to have her watching?
ANNE: She likes to watch people make love . . .
    LAWRENCE*'s trousers come off, he pulls* ANNE *close.*
LAWRENCE: How many people has she watched?
    ANNE *kisses* LAWRENCE *as he holds her.*
ANNE: I've asked, but she's not telling . . .
    ANNE *begins to pull his pants down.* LAWRENCE *is now naked. Suddenly they hear voices from downstairs. They both turn in complete surprise.*

INT. STAIRCASE AND HALL. AFTERNOON.
We cut to ANNE *coming down the stairs, having dressed very hastily, looking a little ruffled.* LAWRENCE *following behind, a couple of buttons on his shirt still undone.*

AUNT ELIZABETH, *a woman in her sixties, is standing at the bottom of the stairs, accompanied by* CELIA.

ANNE: Aunt Elizabeth! What a surprise! I thought you
     were coming tomorrow.
AUNT ELIZABETH: There was a slight change of plan . . .
     She glances at ANNE *and* LAWRENCE *together.*
     Which I hope is not inconvenient.
     CELIA *staring fascinated at* LAWRENCE *and* ANNE.
     Celia was kind enough to meet me at the station.

INT. RECEPTION ROOM. AFTERNOON.
AUNT ELIZABETH *is taking tea in the reception room.* ANNE *and* LAWRENCE *are sitting opposite her.* CELIA *is drinking tea, watching from a corner.* AUNT ELIZABETH *is in full flow.*

AUNT ELIZABETH: It's been quite an extraordinarily busy
     fortnight as it happens, first the ball at Blenheim
     Palace, which I have to admit was spectacular –
     people said it put Versailles to shame – and then there
     was the one at Holland House, which was an awful
     crush and full of politicians and film stars – no
     offence my dear – although the King and Queen did
     put in an appearance . . .
ANNE: Sounds exhausting, Aunt Elizabeth.
AUNT ELIZABETH: Actually it was rather invigorating. (*She
     looks across at* ANNE.) And you're looking very well,
     my dear . . . positively glowing. (*Her gaze moves to*
     LAWRENCE *and then back to* ANNE.) It must be the
     country air . . .

INT./EXT. THE HALL AND FRONT DOOR. DAY.
LAWRENCE *is kissing* ANNE *goodbye, framed at the front door.*

LAWRENCE: I'll see you in London . . .
ANNE: Promise?
LAWRENCE: Of course.
>   *He kisses her.*
>   Even though so much is happening, nothing is going
>   to stop me seeing you. (*He smiles.*)
>   *He leaves. We cut to* ANNE *moving back into the house.*
>   CELIA *is waiting for her at the bottom of the stairs.*
CELIA (*softly*): Let me touch you . . .
>   *She puts her arms around* ANNE.
>   Let me smell you . . . (*She smiles.*) You smell of love . . .
ANNE: Celia . . . !
CELIA (*laughs softly*): I envy you. I ache for a man like that.

INT. ANNE'S DRESSING ROOM. THE FILM STUDIOS. DAY.
ANNE *is sitting in her dressing room at the film studios. She is
in a Regency costume and she is staring at herself in a mirror.
It is a rather shabby room on the back lot overlooking an
unprepossessing yard.*

*In the yard three extras dressed as policemen are having a
smoke, gossiping and playing cards. Behind her in the dressing
room sitting on a moth-eaten sofa is* GILBERT, *a character
actor in late middle age. He is dressed as a Regency country
gentleman. He has a newspaper on his knee.*

GILBERT: You don't mind me doing the crossword here?
ANNE: Of course not, Gilbert.
GILBERT (*watching the police through the window*): They're
>   having much more fun on Stage 2 apparently! *We* won't
>   work today – it is always the bit players that get delayed.
ANNE: Oh come on, no moaning today, Gilbert! I'm really

looking forward to our big scene next week. You are
coming down for the weekend, for the picnic? So we
can rehearse a little?

GILBERT: I'm honoured to be invited, and of course I'm
coming. But I don't really feel we need to rehearse . . .
It is the same old part for me, the jolly old gentleman.
I was a jolly old gentleman when I was twenty-two
and here I am still playing him!

There's a knock at the door and a young man, MICK,
enters without waiting for a reply.

MICK: Phone call, Miss Keyes.

INT. LONG PASSAGE. THE FILM STUDIO. DAY.

ANNE *approaches down a long studio passage, her Regency
dress billowing out.*

*There is a phone on the wall at the end of the passage, its
receiver off waiting for her.* ANNE *picks up the phone.*

LAWRENCE (*voice-over*): It's Lawrence . . .

Hearing his voice, ANNE *smiles delightedly.*

ANNE: Hello!

LAWRENCE (*voice-over*): Have you heard the news?

ANNE: No, what?

LAWRENCE: Hector is dead.

ANNE: What?! . . . What happened? That's terrible.

LAWRENCE: I think he killed himself.

ANNE: Oh my God –

LAWRENCE: It's in the newspaper.

ANNE: I haven't read the newspaper –

LAWRENCE: He must have killed himself or . . . (*He stops.*)

ANNE: Or what?

LAWRENCE: No, I can't talk on the telephone. I am going
to see his parents in Scotland, I'll find out more. As
soon as I'm back, we'll –

ANNE: How long are you going for?

LAWRENCE: Not long . . . When I'm back I have to see you.

ANNE: I have to see you too.

  LAWRENCE's *voice suddenly very hushed, confidential.*

LAWRENCE: Anne?

ANNE: Yes . . . what?

LAWRENCE: No, we can't do this now . . . I'll see you when I return –

ANNE: I'll miss you. Is there a number you can give me? So I can reach you?

LAWRENCE: I'll see when I get there . . . I've got to go now.

  The phone clicks off.

  A wide shot of ANNE *standing in her long dress in the dark passage.*

INT. ANNE'S DRESSING ROOM. DAY.

ANNE *moves back into her dressing room.* GILBERT *looks up.*

GILBERT: Ah, there you are! I thought for a moment you'd been called and gone without me. (*Seeing her shocked face.*) What's the matter?

ANNE: Somebody I know has died. (*She glances across.*) It's in the paper.

  We cut to ANNE *turning the pages of the newspaper, trying to find the story. We see headlines of that day, a jumble of European news and trivial home stories. All the headlines are the same size.*

  We see 'MEMBER OF PARLIAMENT FOUND DEAD'.

  ANNE *gives the newspaper to* GILBERT. *She moves to the window. The policemen extras are now playing football in the yard, laughing and shouting together. One of them grins at her.*

GILBERT (*glancing at the story*): Oh yes, Hector Haldane,

always thought he had a marvellous name, he was
one of the young Members of Parliament who was
speaking out against appeasing Herr Hitler. I read one
of his speeches – passionate stuff – he's been calling
for a change at the top, for a new Prime Minister.
(*He looks up.*) How sad – he was a man of potential.

ANNE: I saw him only a couple of weeks ago.

INT. THE NORFOLK HOUSE. NIGHT.
AUNT ELIZABETH, ALEXANDER, MAUD, RALPH *and* CELIA
*are standing in the hall of the Norfolk house in their overcoats,
preparing to go out. They look very smart, only* CELIA *is not
wearing a coat.*
    ANNE *enters the darkened hall.*

AUNT ELIZABETH: There you are my dear! We thought you
    weren't coming.
ANNE: I'm sorry I am late. It is such a long journey from
    the studio.
RALPH (*quietly*): And now you've got a thrilling evening
    to look forward to, meeting our new vicar . . . and
    it's some sort of anniversary for the village, which
    everyone's taking very seriously!
ANNE (*to Alexander*): Have you heard the news?
ALEXANDER (*with feeling*): We have. Poor Hector. It's terrible
    news. He was so full of life.

EXT. THE VILLAGE STREET. NIGHT.
*The family is walking through the main street of the village at
night. The street is lined by ancient cottages.*
    *The few villagers they pass all stand very respectfully as the
family walk by, the men doffing their caps, the women nodding.*

The three siblings running towards the abbey.

Walter and Oliver tell Michael the story of Anne.

Lawrence and Anne at the abbey before war has begun.

Hector's outburst at the dinner attacking appeasement.

Balcombe watching Hector during the dinner.

Alexander reassures a distraught Anne during the search for the baby.

Ralph and Celia having been up all night at the Ball.

The sleeping girls the day after the Ball.

Gilbert's message to Anne during the recording session.

Aunt Elizabeth and Anne listen to the choir.

Anne is reunited with her father at the Foreign Office.

Anne discovers Lawrence's body among the dead animals at the vet's.

Alexander looking for Anne on the common.

Anne takes the drink from her father.

Anne locked in Aunt Elizabeth's house.

The family watch Anne as she runs away.

AUNT ELIZABETH (*seeing the villagers paying their respects*):
    I'm glad to see some things don't change. The family
    still matters here, clearly . . .
    ALEXANDER *acknowledges the villagers as the family*
    process to church. CELIA *is hunched against the cold.*
ANNE (*as if she is used to ordering her around*): You should
    have put on a coat, Celia, no wonder you are cold.
    CELIA *looks up at the sharpness of* ANNE*'s tone.*
ALEXANDER (*seeing* ANNE *very preoccupied*): Of course you're
    shocked, my dear. Do you know what happened?
ANNE: No. Lawrence didn't tell me very much. He said he
    thought Hector had killed himself.
ALEXANDER: It's possible, he was rather excitable. But
    there was something very touching about him.
ANNE: And very brave.

INT. THE CHURCH. NIGHT.
We cut to the interior of the medieval church, lit with a mixture
of electric light and candles. It is entirely empty except for the
family. AUNT ELIZABETH, ALEXANDER, MAUD *and the siblings*
are sitting in the family pews at the front of the church. Slightly
to one side is ALEXANDER*'s sister* KATHLEEN, *who is sitting*
with a toddler, the one-year-old OLIVER, *on her knees. The only*
other people in the church are a group of choristers standing in
the choir stalls, a group of angelic-looking boys dressed in bright
blue surplices. The VICAR, *a tubby man with a smooth baby*
face, is approaching the family very respectfully.

AUNT ELIZABETH (*in a loud whisper*): Let us hope he is an
    improvement on the last one . . .
VICAR (*addressing the family*): I am so honoured you were
    able to come this evening!
ALEXANDER: While I am delighted we are getting our own
    private performance.

AUNT ELIZABETH: And we're *all here*.

ALEXANDER: This is my Aunt Elizabeth, the sister of my
    dear late mother –

AUNT ELIZABETH *nods graciously.*

– and my wife Maud –

MAUD *gives the vicar a tiny distant smile.*

– and you've already met my sister Kathleen, of
    course, her boy is in the choir.

We see the YOUNG WALTER, *a boy of twelve, staring out
of the choir at the family.*

VICAR: Oh yes . . . (*Turning to the siblings.*) And these are
    your children? (*He looks at* ANNE.) This must be the
    eldest . . .

ANNE *smiles at him. The* VICAR *turns to* RALPH *and*
CELIA.

And *these* then are the children.

ANNE *looks surprised at the* VICAR*'s tone, as if* RALPH
and CELIA *are the genuine children.*

VICAR: We're nearly ready to start. I do hope you approve,
    I'm conducting the choir myself today . . . It's an
    anthem that reaches back almost as far as your family!
    He approaches the choir.

ALEXANDER (*amused smile to* ANNE): He's just as I expected
    him to be . . .

CELIA: Are we allowed to wave at Walter?

ALEXANDER (*seeing* ANNE *very preoccupied*): You're still
    looking so pale, my dear.

ANNE: Yes . . . I was just thinking about Hector . . . He
    must have been under a lot of pressure because of his
    views, mustn't he?

ALEXANDER: Yes, but of course he was not the only one
    saying those things.

ANNE (*staring out towards the choristers*): I was also
    wondering about Mr Balcombe . . . What does he do,
    Papa?

ALEXANDER: He works at the Home Office doing various
things.

RALPH (*breezily*): He is in the Secret Service of course,
that's obvious.

ANNE: He is? . . . Would he have taken an interest in Hector?

RALPH: Very possibly – but I don't think he can have
bumped him off, Anne!

CELIA: Bumped him off?! Oh Anne, your love of the
dramatic!

ANNE: No, I didn't mean that, of course –

CELIA: Mind you, he is quite spooky . . .

ALEXANDER: He seems a little odd, I admit. (*He smiles.*)
But he shares my love of fishing.

ANNE: It's only . . . Hector seemed worried about him –

ALEXANDER (*to* ANNE, *softly*): You can't just get rid of
Members of Parliament like that . . . (*He smiles.*)
I hope.

*The choir begins to sing an Elizabethan anthem by
William Byrd.* YOUNG WALTER *stares across at the family
as he sings. He is a very solemn-looking child.* ANNE *stares
back at the choir as the boys sing. We are close on her eyes.
The music soars.*

For a moment we see HECTOR *gesticulating, holding
forth as* BALCOMBE *watches him from the other end of the
table on the night of the birthday.*

ALEXANDER (*very close, as if reading* ANNE*'s thoughts*): I'll
ask Mr Balcombe to move all the stuff he's got stored
in our sheds; it's not right that we have things round
the house and we don't know what they are.

ANNE (*softly as the choir sings*): Yes, I think that would be a
very good idea.

ALEXANDER: He can do it very soon . . . he is coming to
the picnic. (*He smiles.*) We will feed him up and then
get him to take everything away.

We are on ANNE*'s eyes as the choir sings.*

EXT. FIELD AND WOODS. DAY.

We cut to a wide shot of the picnic, the family spread out in the shade of some trees on the side of a gentle slope overlooking a valley. There are decorative rugs, fine china, picnic baskets.
AUNT ELIZABETH *is sitting in a bath chair,* RALPH *and* CELIA *are lolling on the grass,* MAUD *is gazing at the wild flowers,* GILBERT *is sitting drinking a lot of red wine.* ALEXANDER *is lying on a rug nonchalantly smoking a cigar, his sister* KATHLEEN *is sitting with her two children, baby* OLIVER, *who is in a smart pushchair, and* YOUNG WALTER, *who is sitting, very watchful, drinking lemonade. The atmosphere is hazy and replete. In the middle of them all is* BALCOMBE, *who is sitting upright, his legs crossed.* ANNE *is lying on the ground, as far away as possible from* BALCOMBE, *drinking wine. She is very unsettled by* BALCOMBE'*s presence, his dark eyes.*

GILBERT (*well oiled with drink*): What a splendid estate you have here – no wonder you're so proud of it, Sir Alexander! I remember hearing you speak at a public meeting about the wonders of nature and the importance of beauty in our lives – it was inspiring, I thought about it for days!

ALEXANDER: It's marvellous somebody actually remembers what one said. (*Self-deprecating smile.*) It hardly ever happens.

RALPH (*playful smile at his father*): In fact never!

GILBERT: And your book on Disraeli is an absolute classic of course. I've read it twice . . .

AUNT ELIZABETH (*to the boy* WALTER): Walter, I am being lazy, too full of food, can you move me a fraction, so I can see this famous view a little better?
We watch for a moment as YOUNG WALTER *wheels the old lady in the bath chair, his serious face staring ahead as he does so.*

ANNE *cannot stop herself watching* BALCOMBE *as he eats; he is carefully peeling a boiled egg. He is sitting very straight, a formidable, silent presence in the middle of this family picnic.*

AUNT ELIZABETH (*to* GILBERT): You are right, Mr Williams, it is a very untouched part of the world, for the moment at least. I know I've seen you in the theatre many times . . . and one or two performances really stood out, your Porter in *Macbeth*, for instance.

GILBERT: Ah yes, a particularly drunk porter I remember – especially towards the end of the week!

BALCOMBE *notices* ANNE *watching him. He stares straight at her.*

BALCOMBE: Is it interesting, the part you are playing? (*He carefully folds his napkin.*) In the film you're currently making?

ANNE: Yes, I think it is . . . She is rather ambitious, and quite plucky really.

BALCOMBE: Acting . . . ! What fun that must be, dressing up and being different people. (*He sips his wine.*) Deciding each day who you are going to be . . . and who you're going to turn into next.

GILBERT *rolls his eyes at this. Suddenly* RALPH *leaps up.*

RALPH: Come on, everybody . . . ! We've got to walk off all this food. Let's go to the mossy island . . .

CELIA: Why do we have to? I can't move!

But they begin to stand up. BALCOMBE *brushing the grass off his smart trousers.*

ALEXANDER: We can't take the baby to the mossy island . . .

AUNT ELIZABETH: That's all right, I will stay here and look after it.

ANNE: No, Aunt Elizabeth . . . you don't have to do that. I can stay here . . . study my lines.

She indicates her script lying on the grass.

AUNT ELIZABETH: We'll sit and look after him together.

> ALEXANDER *tenderly, attentively, adjusts* AUNT
> ELIZABETH's *shawl. Then we cut to* ANNE's *point of view
> as she watches the family move away towards the wood.
> All of them have gone, including* WALTER *and*
> BALCOMBE, *leaving just* AUNT ELIZABETH *sitting in the
> bath chair, the baby* OLIVER *in his pushchair and* ANNE.
>
> ANNE *takes another sip of wine and exchanges a look
> with* OLIVER.

AUNT ELIZABETH (*swatting a wasp away*): If you don't mind,
my dear, I think I might stretch my legs after all – I'm
going to lose all use of them if I don't get out of this
ridiculous chair at once. (*As she gets up.*) And I object
to being a free meal for these insects!

> *We cut to* ANNE *and the baby alone together. The sound of
> the grasshoppers chirping away, their noise increasing all
> the time.* ANNE *can hear the sound of laughter and voices
> of the family fading away among the trees. We move in on
> her eyes.*
>
> *An abrupt cut to shots of* ANNE *and* LAWRENCE
> *passionately kissing. She is kissing his bare chest, he is
> kissing her shoulders, touching her lips, holding her close,
> his arms wrapped around her.*
>
> ANNE's *eyes suddenly spring open. She sits up startled,
> realising she must have dozed off for a few seconds. She
> looks round. We cut wide. We see she is completely alone.*
>
> *There is no sign of* OLIVER *or the pushchair.*

ANNE: Oliver?! (*She spins round, she calls out.*) Hello . . . ?!
(*Urgently.*) They must have come back for him . . .

> *She starts running towards the edge of the wood.*

Hello? . . . Hello?! . . . Have you got Oliver with you?!

> *She reaches the edge of the wood and starts running along
> the path that leads through the wood. As she runs she is
> calling all the time.*

Hello?! ... Ralph?! ... Celia?! ... Kathleen?! Can you
hear me? ... HAVE YOU GOT OLIVER? Hello ... ?!
She is looking at the ground for any sign of OLIVER *and
then all around. She lets out a really enormous shout.*
Hello, can you hear me?!
She rounds a corner in the path.
     There in front of her is YOUNG WALTER *standing stock
still in the middle of the path.*

ANNE: Walter?! Didn't you hear me?!

YOUNG WALTER: Yes. I heard you.

ANNE: Have they got Oliver with them?!

YOUNG WALTER: No, you've got Oliver.

ANNE: No, he's gone. Somebody must have come back for
him when I wasn't looking.

YOUNG WALTER: He is not on the mossy island ... I have
just been there ...
     At that moment ANNE *hears a crunch among the branches
back along the path, the area she has just come from. She
thinks she sees a fleeting movement in the trees. She yells.*

ANNE: Hello ... ? Who's that?
     She turns back to YOUNG WALTER, *who is staring at her
impassively.*
Did you see that? I think ... there is somebody there –

YOUNG WALTER: I didn't see.

ANNE: Walter, go and get them all back. Right now – go
on! We've got to look for him ...
     The boy hesitates.
Go on, Walter – get them all back here. *Quick!*
ANNE *moves off, back along the path towards where she
heard the noise.*
     *She stops suddenly. There on the path is a toddler's little
shoe, the same path she came along a moment before. She
picks up the shoe and rushes on through the wood.*
     *She comes out of the wood and finds herself at the edge
of the abbey.*

She stops again; she can just make out the faint sound
of a toddler's cry coming from among the ruins. She calls.
Oliver!
She moves among the pillars of the abbey towards the
gatehouse. She can hear the sound of the toddler crying,
still very faint but it is increasing.

    As she gets near the gatehouse she suddenly sees a
movement, a dark suited figure glimpsed on the upper
parapet. It is so fleeting, she only sees it for a moment.

    She plunges up the stone spiral staircase that leads to
the top of the gatehouse.

    The crying is getting louder. She yells.

ANNE: Oliver?!

The crying is louder still. And then it suddenly stops. There
is complete silence, just the sound of the wind.

    At the top of the gatehouse there is a stone chamber. She
runs into it. It is empty. ANNE *turns, alone in the stone*
room. Then she hears a sound from the base of the
gatehouse, a baby crying, urgent and loud. She hurtles
back down the steps.

    As she reaches the bottom, she shouts in surprise,
spinning backwards, as a face is staring at her through the
lattice window at the bottom of the stairs. It moves back
into the shadows and vanishes. ANNE *runs out of the*
gatehouse and round the corner on to the path. She finds
YOUNG WALTER *standing there.*

ANNE (*furious*): Walter?! What are you doing here? I told
    you to fetch them all!

YOUNG WALTER: I've done that. They're all coming back.
    (*He looks at her.*) I came to help.

ANNE (*staring back into the child's eyes*): Are you playing a
    game, Walter?

YOUNG WALTER: No, I am not playing a game.

ANNE (*catching hold of him*): Did you move Oliver? Did
    somebody tell you to play a game?

YOUNG WALTER (*meeting her gaze*): I told you I am not
  playing a game.

ANNE (*holding on to him really tight, her tone really forceful*):
  Where is Oliver?! Come on – I think you know –
  where is he?! TELL ME WHERE HE IS?!
  *She looks up. The whole family is approaching her across
  the field, seeing her holding the child, forcibly interrogating
  him.* BALCOMBE *is walking slightly apart from the others.*
      ANNE *begins to run towards them. They don't seem to
  have the toddler with them.*

ANNE: Have you got Oliver?!

RALPH: We haven't –

ANNE: He's gone! I was just there – I turned round . . . he
  was gone . . . and the pushchair – just vanished . . .

ALEXANDER: Calm down, Anne . . . He can't have gone far –

AUNT ELIZABETH: He was just sitting quietly when I left . . .

ALEXANDER: He may have just slipped out of his chair.

ANNE: But they've taken the pushchair and everything . . . !

KATHLEEN: Oh my God!
  She sees BALCOMBE *studying her closely and* GILBERT
  too, all of them seeing her on the verge of total panic.
      KATHLEEN *is staring at her really accusingly.*

ANNE: If you haven't got him – somebody has taken him!
  (*She holds out the shoes.*) I found his shoe . . .

ALEXANDER: What?!

BALCOMBE (*with quiet authority*): We will all look for him,
  back at the picnic site. If we all fan out . . . we can
  cover a lot of ground between us.
  ANNE *is beside herself with panic. She moves towards her
  father.*

ANNE: I'm so sorry . . . I'm so sorry . . .

ALEXANDER: It'll be all right, darling.
  We cut back to the picnic site. The family and BALCOMBE
  *are spread out along the rim of the wood, moving slowly
  through the edge of the trees.*

CELIA (*moving through the undergrowth*): He can't have got out and pushed the chair himself can he?

ALEXANDER: He won't have gone far . . .

BALCOMBE (*suddenly taking* ANNE *by the arm*): I think we should take this path, Anne . . .

ANNE very startled that BALCOMBE *has grasped her arm, although he is not rough with her. He is guiding her along the path through the wood. He is very close to her.*

ANNE: I've looked here! Of course this was the first place I looked . . . I went along this path . . .

ALEXANDER, CELIA *and* RALPH *catch* ANNE *and* BALCOMBE *up.* BALCOMBE *now drops back a few paces, so he is behind them.*

ANNE: He wasn't anywhere here . . . I looked . . . He's *not* here . . . !

She rounds the corner. Facing her in the middle of the path is the pushchair with OLIVER *sitting in it, staring back at them.*

Oh thank God! (*She turns.*) But he wasn't here when I looked . . .

RALPH: We've found him . . . Everybody, we've found him!

ANNE sees BALCOMBE *staring at her.*

KATHLEEN *comes running, followed by* WALTER, GILBERT, MAUD *and* AUNT ELIZABETH.

ALEXANDER: Here he is! Safe and sound! The panic's over.

ALEXANDER *lifts* OLIVER *up gently and gives him to* KATHLEEN.

AUNT ELIZABETH: How on earth did he get here?

ANNE: I don't know. I really don't know! I must have fallen asleep for a few seconds – and he was gone. Somebody moved him . . .

RALPH: Somebody moved him?!

CELIA: Maybe you were concentrating so much on your lines, darling, going over them in your head, you walked with him without realising.

ANNE: I didn't walk with him! I didn't move him!

BALCOMBE: Are you sure about that? You said you fell
     asleep –

ANNE (*furious, staring at* BALCOMBE): I didn't walk with
     him! I didn't move him . . . I am absolutely certain of
     that.
     *They are all staring at her. She can see the disbelief in
     their eyes.*
     I DID NOT MOVE HIM!

INT. NORFOLK HOUSE. RECEPTION ROOM. EVENING.
ALEXANDER, ANNE *and* CELIA *are sitting in a window seat in
the reception room, overlooking the front drive. It is evening,
a few hours after the picnic. Through the window we can see*
BALCOMBE *supervising two men assembling packing cases in
a pile in the drive, ready to be taken away.* RALPH *is standing
close to the window, watching too.*

ALEXANDER (*staring at the boxes in the drive*): He did have a
     hell of a lot packed away in our sheds!

RALPH: I hear they've got the Duke of Wellington to take
     several tons of confidential material and put it in his
     basement! They are so worried about Communist
     infiltration at the Foreign Office they'd rather put it
     in a duke's wine cellar!

CELIA: And with us. (*Watching* BALCOMBE *through the
     window.*) What excuse did you give, Papa, to make
     him take it all away?

ALEXANDER: I said in winter the sheds all leak. He seemed
     quite happy with that!
     ANNE *is sitting quiet, staring at* BALCOMBE *intensely.*

ANNE: I didn't move the baby . . . You ought to believe me.

ALEXANDER (*taking her hand*): I do believe you.

CELIA: Then who moved him?

ANNE: It was Walter.

RALPH: Walter . . . ? Why would he do that?

ALEXANDER: Maybe it was the boy, who knows? Perhaps
he had had a glass of wine when we weren't looking.
(*Softly, to* ANNE.) Wine and the sun can do funny
things . . .

ANNE (*ignoring this, watching* BALCOMBE): Or somebody
asked him to move him.

CELIA *following her look through the window.* BALCOMBE
is a commanding presence in the drive.

CELIA: Why would he do that, darling?

ANNE: To make me seem unreliable . . . a bit dotty.

RALPH: But he doesn't know you were the one that made
him take all his lovely boxes away . . .

ANNE (*watching* BALCOMBE): He knows I am friends with
Lawrence and Hector . . .

ALEXANDER *follows her look.*

ALEXANDER: All things are possible . . . although that
would be a very strange thing to do. (*Gently but
firmly.*) But I think we should let Mr Balcombe
disappear with all his boxes, don't you, and just not
invite him again. (*Watching him.*) Ever.

BALCOMBE *is now approaching them, walking towards
the house. His sharp handsome face looking at them
through the window.*

ALEXANDER: We want to make sure we get rid of him . . .
which I am sure we can do.

RALPH (*staring at the boxes*): We've lost a terrific chance to
do a lot of snooping –

BALCOMBE *appears in the doorway.*

BALCOMBE: So – I think we've got everything.

ANNE (*unable to resist*): Including all the foxtrots?

BALCOMBE (*completely unfazed by this*): I believe so, yes.

He stares at the family. He stands very still. He seems to
dominate the room.

And there's nothing left behind in here, is there? In
the house?

ALEXANDER: I don't believe so, Joseph. No.

BALCOMBE *looks straight at* ANNE. *Their eyes meet.*

ANNE: No. I don't know of anything.

INT. ANNE'S BEDROOM. NIGHT.

We can hear dance music from downstairs. We cut to ANNE
*opening a drawer in her bedroom. Under a pile of sweaters are
the two remaining gramophone records she took from the shed.*

  There is a knock on the door. She slips the drawer shut.

ANNE: Come in.

  CELIA *comes into the room. Sonia is sitting on* ANNE*'s bed.*

CELIA: Just wanted to see how you are?

ANNE (*sharp*): I am absolutely fine . . . there's nothing
  wrong with me.

CELIA: Of course not. (*Airily.*) Just think of it as – you
  simply fell asleep, darling, even if that's not what
  happened!

  She looks pointedly at ANNE.

  You were probably having the most wonderful dream,
  weren't you, when it happened?

  ANNE *looks surprised.* CELIA *smiles.*

  No need to tell me! (*She moves over to the cat.*)

  Anyway, the spooky man has gone at last, and Papa
  says we're going back to London tomorrow morning!

ANNE: Really?

CELIA (*stroking Sonia*): Because Parliament may be about
  to be recalled. There is a bit of a crisis apparently –
  but I think it's terrific we're going, nowadays I can't
  stand it down here after a couple of weeks. And with
  no disrespect to Sonia (*to the cat*) – and I am sure
  you'll forgive me, won't you – I really miss Horatio . . .

INT. THE LONDON HOUSE. AFTERNOON.

We cut to the grand staircase of the London house. In the middle of the stairs, sitting in splendid isolation, is a white cat, Horatio.

We cut to a high-angled shot of the hall looking towards the front door. We see the shutters all closed and the furniture draped in dust sheets.

The family, ALEXANDER, MAUD, CELIA, RALPH *and* ANNE, *enter the hall, throwing shadows in the gloom across the floor.* ANNE *is holding her bag quite tightly. A maid,* BETTY, *is running to greet them. From next door we can hear a lot of banging and voices.*

BETTY: Oh, Sir Alexander, I wasn't expecting you! The house is not aired! And Mrs Hardiman is not back till the end of the week. I am so sorry . . .

ALEXANDER: No need to alarm yourself, Betty. It's not your fault we live in unpredictable times . . .

MAUD: We can manage without Mrs Hardiman.

BETTY: And there is this awful racket from next door sir . . . They are getting ready for a party! There's been banging all day long!

MAUD: I am sure it will all be fine . . . just so long as they don't throw anything into our garden.

RALPH: And remember to invite us!

> CELIA *has moved up the stairs and picked up Horatio. She stares down at them with the white cat in her arms.* BETTY *is moving to start taking the dust sheets off.*

ALEXANDER: No, don't change anything, Betty. Leave everything as it is. Who knows what will happen in the next few days?

INT. ANNE'S LONDON BEDROOM. DAY.

We cut to ANNE *dropping her bag on to her bed. The room is very austere, her bedroom furniture is covered in dust sheets, the*

blinds are shut. ANNE *takes out the two gramophone records
from her bag. As she does so dance music starts drifting up from
downstairs. She slips the records back into the bag just as*
RALPH *bangs through the door.*

RALPH: It doesn't seem to be our home at all, does it, the
house all wrapped up like this?

ANNE: No, it feels like maybe absolutely everything is
about to change.

RALPH *throws himself on to the bed and stares up at the
ceiling.*

RALPH: The FO will be abuzz, which means they will
actually get to work at eleven o'clock in the morning –
which is when we are meant to start working, would
you believe – rather than drifting in at eleven thirty!

RALPH *props himself up on his elbow, looks at* ANNE.
Glorious, I know this is a very sensitive subject, but
with my new job I have access to all sorts of things . . .
and I know who to ask to find out even more – so,
only if you wish it, of course, but I could find out who
your real parents were?

ANNE *turns, very surprised.*

ANNE: You could?

RALPH: So what do you think? I know you asked Papa
once and of course he didn't know . . . Only if you
really wish it, Glorious.

ANNE (*thoughtful*): I don't know if I want to know . . . It's
never really worried me for some reason who my real
parents are. I don't think about it much any more.
(*She turns.*) It's a big decision.

INT. HALL AND PASSAGE. LONDON HOUSE. AFTERNOON.
We cut to ANNE *moving across the hall carrying the two
gramophone records in their brown sleeves. Through a half-open*

door she can see CELIA *in the reception room standing with her back to* ANNE *listening to a record on the gramophone. We can hear the banging and the voices from next door. The only furniture we can see is still covered in dust sheets.* BETTY *is coming down the passage towards* ANNE.

ANNE: There was another gramophone, wasn't there,
　　　Betty, an old wind-up one? What happened to that?
BETTY: Oh that old thing, miss, I put it away in the lumber
　　　room.

INT. LUMBER ROOM. AFTERNOON.
We cut to blackness, the door of the lumber room opening towards us and ANNE *entering it. The lumber room is full of old boxes, broken furniture and wellington boots. In among all this is an old wind-up gramophone.* ANNE *moves with difficulty in the confined space; old bed springs spike her; she gets to the gramophone.*
　　We cut to ANNE *heaving the gramophone on to a small table. The only space for it is directly in front of the door. She is alone inside the lumber room with the door shut.*
　　We cut to the needle going on to the first record.
　　We hear an official-sounding voice chairing a meeting. ANNE *doesn't recognise the voice; it is not* BALCOMBE.

VOICE: We are clear which sectors are being concentrated
　　　on and which sectors remain still to be enquired into?
　　　The recording is partly inaudible. ANNE *moves the needle
　　　along the record, the voice is droning on.*
VOICE: I think we are all agreed which areas are the
　　　highest priority . . . The reports that we have had back
　　　so far are to be studied at the next meeting . . . The
　　　individual reports we will be looking into are numbers
　　　10, 15 and 22; 37 is still being completed . . .

ANNE *rolls her eyes at the droning voice. She takes the*
record off.

We cut to the needle dropping on to the second record.
Immediately the record starts we hear a voice shrieking,
a truly unnerving sound; the individual is desperate.

VOICE: I told you . . . You keep ringing me . . . and you've
got to stop, YOU'VE GOT TO STOP THIS.

ANNE*'s eyes widen. She recognises the voice. She is*
crouching by the gramophone.

ANNE: Hector . . .

A second voice which ANNE *doesn't recognise is chivvying*
HECTOR *with a quietly insinuating tone.*

SECOND VOICE: We are just reminding you, Mr Haldane,
of the information we possess, and we think that
information is of genuine interest to certain people –

HECTOR (*his voice hysterical*): I know the information
you've got, and that information is *private* – don't you
understand that, it's PRIVATE . . . People do all sorts
of things in their lives, everybody knows that! – And if
I have, I have! – I just want you to stop calling me
and my parents. You tried to call my parents and that
is *unforgivable.*

We are on ANNE*'s face as she listens to the desperate tone*
in HECTOR*'s voice. She is shocked and moved.*

SECOND VOICE: We only wanted you to realise we meant
what we said, and it is best for you to listen to us . . .

HECTOR (*truly screaming, furious and terrified*): I am sorry,
I just cannot believe, I *cannot* believe this is happening
to me . . . I want you to stop calling my parents, do
you hear me?! (*Screams.*) DO YOU HEAR ME?! You
have to agree to that – my father is ill . . . he cannot
stand it. You have no right, no right at all to do any of
this. Do you hear me?! You have to stop. YOU HAVE
TO STOP.

At that moment the door of the lumber room opens and the

*gramophone crashes off the small table, smashing the
record.*

BETTY *is standing there, staring down at* ANNE, *very
surprised to see her crouching on her knees on the floor of
the lumber room.*

BETTY: I am so sorry, miss, I had no idea you were in
here . . . I didn't realise you meant you were going to
listen to something in here!

ANNE (*trying to remain as composed as possible*): Don't worry
Betty, it's my fault. Just had to listen to something for
the part I am playing in the film . . . the director gave
it to me, and I wanted somewhere private . . .

BETTY *picks up the shattered record.*

BETTY: And now I've broken it . . . Shall I throw it away
miss?

ANNE: Yes, of course. (*She smiles.*) It's no use like that.

ANNE *is holding the remaining intact record. She moves
out of the lumber room.*

INT. THE MAIN HALL AND STAIRCASE. LATE AFTERNOON.
We cut to ANNE, *still very shaken, walking back towards the
hall. The banging has stopped from next door. Late-afternoon
sun is throwing long shadows.*

ALEXANDER: Hello darling . . .

ANNE *looks up. Her father is standing at the top of the
stairs. He is in a dinner jacket and looks very debonair.*

ANNE *is standing at the bottom of the stairs holding the
gramophone record in its brown sleeve.*

ANNE: Going out, Papa?

ALEXANDER: Yes, to the club. (*He smiles.*) Where the
atmosphere will be feverish, I am sure.

ANNE (*softly*): I need to talk to you . . . when you have a
moment.

ALEXANDER: Not now, darling, there have been developments . . . (*He smiles down at her.*) The world goes on moving faster and faster and I am not at all sure we can stop that.

He stares down at ANNE *holding the record.*

ALEXANDER: More gramophone records, I see?

ANNE: Yes . . .

ALEXANDER (*more stern*): I thought you gave everything back to Mr Balcombe? What is that?

ANNE *suddenly feels reluctant to confess in the middle of the hall when her father is in a hurry.*

ANNE: Oh, this is a real foxtrot for once . . .

ALEXANDER: Is it? Good. (*He looks straight at her.*) We don't want to give Mr Balcombe an excuse to return.

ANNE: I know.

ALEXANDER *moves down the stairs towards her.*

ANNE: That would not be good . . . no.

ALEXANDER (*softly*): We'll talk when this crisis is over . . . (*Taking her arm.*) Where is that handsome new friend of yours?

ANNE: He is away at the moment.

ALEXANDER: You will be happier when he is back.

He kisses her.

INT. THE RECEPTION ROOM. LATE AFTERNOON.
We cut to RALPH *by the gramophone, playing dance music. He turns on seeing* ANNE *in the doorway. The banging and voices from next door have restarted.*

RALPH: I love them having a party next door as the balloon is going up!

ANNE: Is the balloon going up? Now? I should have been listening to the wireless more –

RALPH (*breezily*): It may or may not be going up . . .
Should we be held to our promise to Poland? Do we
really want to go to war for them? Can this be
happening all over again? That's what's going on!
They're all travelling back from their country estates
as we speak, it's as bad as that!
ANNE *looks very preoccupied.* RALPH *smiles.*
Nothing you can do, Glorious, you go on making
your movie – cheer people up!

ANNE: I can't just do that, I've got to do more.

RALPH (*firmly, real authority*): No, Glorious, this is good
advice. (*He looks across at her.*) It's an absolutely
splendid thing to cheer people up!

INT. THE STUDIO. THE SOUND STAGE. DAY.
The dark, empty sound stage. In the distance we see GILBERT
is sitting in his Regency costume on a chair, looking despondent.
His face lights up when he sees ANNE *approach. She is again*
in her Regency dress.

GILBERT: There you are!

ANNE: What do you mean? I have been looking for you
everywhere!

GILBERT: I had so little to do I wandered in here.

ANNE: It's not going to be today, our scene, they've told us
to go.

GILBERT: Not today! I don't believe it! We will never be
needed . . .

ANNE: The weather's not right, they say . . . I've managed
to get my father's chauffeur to come and collect us.
Would you come home with me, Gilbert?

GILBERT: How could anyone resist such an invitation?!

ANNE: I've got something I want to play you – in private.
She indicates the record in its brown sleeve in her bag.

This gramophone record . . . (*She smiles.*) You are so
much better informed about everything than I am –
GILBERT: Flattery as well, today is definitely looking up!
ANNE: We've got to stop off somewhere though, to pick up
my brother and sister – they have been to a ball.
GILBERT: Oh have they! (*Smiling fondly at her.*) Why
weren't you at this ball, Anne?
ANNE (*laughs*): Because I thought I was going to be working
with you – and as you know I take our big scene
together very seriously, unlike you!

INT. THE LIMOUSINE. AFTERNOON.
GILBERT *and* ANNE *are sitting together, in their normal clothes,
on the back seat of a Daimler limousine. They are surrounded by
mahogany, folding seats, a drinks cabinet, a luxurious interior.
They are being driven by a uniformed chauffeur,* DAWSON, *a
tall, impassive figure.* ANNE *is watching his face in the driving
mirror.*

GILBERT: This is the way to travel for a poor boy like me!
Always dreamt I would get a car like this as an actor –
it hasn't happened yet! I never got above the title, not
even once!
For a moment GILBERT*'s face expresses intense melancholy.
The decanters are rattling in the drinks cabinet.* GILBERT
is eyeing them.
ANNE: Help yourself, Gilbert, please.
GILBERT *immediately brightens. He leans forward,
inspects the contents of the cabinet.*
GILBERT: Marvellous . . . two sorts of sherry, cigars – what
more could one ask? You've got to join me, Anne . . .
*We cut wide outside the car. We see it is travelling down a
leafy empty road towards London, as we hear* GILBERT*'s
voice.*

GILBERT (*voice-over*): It's time for some riotous living
    because one has no idea what is going to happen
    tomorrow!
    We cut back inside the car, the air thick with cigar smoke.
    ANNE *and* GILBERT *are drinking,* GILBERT *is smoking a*
    big cigar and ANNE *a cigarette.*
GILBERT: So what is the tune you want to play me?
ANNE: It's not a tune . . . It's a conversation.
    She see's DAWSON*'s face in the mirror. She leans forward*
    and slides the glass partition shut.
ANNE: It's a recording of a meeting. I found it among the
    things Mr Balcombe was storing with us in Norfolk.
    There was another record as well, of Hector screaming,
    really upset –
GILBERT: The man who killed himself? Where is it? I would
    like to hear that –
ANNE: It's broken, it got smashed.
    GILBERT *gives* ANNE *a very sceptical look as she drinks.*
ANNE: I know since the baby and the pushchair you don't
    trust what I say, Gilbert –
GILBERT (*mock innocent*): When did I say that?
ANNE (*taking another sip of drink*): – and I know it's my
    fault I haven't read more about the political situation,
    been too bound up in my work – but it's conceivable,
    isn't it, that the Secret Service are listening in and
    recording the conversations of those that are opposed
    to the government – that's possible?
GILBERT (*refilling his glass*): Well, my dear, I am just an old
    actor and therefore nothing I say is of any value –
ANNE: That's not true, you are the best-informed person
    I know!
GILBERT: – but I would have thought it is extremely
    possible.
ANNE: Yes . . . and obviously that spying and those
    recordings could be used to put pressure on people,

couldn't they? To blackmail them into silence if
necessary?

GILBERT (*less sure about this*): That too is possible, if risky –

ANNE: Yes, risky because they wouldn't want that to
become public under any circumstances?

GILBERT: Of course not! Just imagine what the supporters
of Winston Churchill would do with information like
that – it would bring down the present leadership
immediately . . . Churchill would become Prime
Minister and that would lead to a far bolder and more
aggressive approach to Germany!

He puffs on his cigar and gives a chuckle.

Blackmail . . . well I never.

He takes another puff, more thoughtful.

But it's always possible elements in the Secret Service
are taking things further than the Prime Minister
intended . . . much further than they were meant to.

ANNE (*watching Dawson in the mirror*): Do you think Mr
Churchill's phone calls are being listened in to?

GILBERT: Could be . . . (*He grins: he is well oiled with drink
now.*) Perhaps we should tell him! (*Not really believing
her.*) Is that what you've got on that recording of
yours?

ANNE: No, no. It's merely a boring meeting, but perhaps
you'll know who the people are . . . (*She refills her
glass.*) Why would they record a boring meeting?

GILBERT (*taking a puff of his cigar*): Maybe because
somebody couldn't be there and they didn't want any
notes to be taken –

ANNE: Yes –

GILBERT (*grins*): That's just a slightly drunken actor's
guess, of course!

ANNE: But now, if war comes, none of this matters.

GILBERT: Who told you that?

ANNE: Nobody told me that . . . I am working it out –

GILBERT: On the contrary, dear, it will matter all the more.
(*Expansive with drink.*) Some of these people – like
the ones who made your recordings – they don't want
a war, they certainly don't want Winston Churchill
as Prime Minister, they want this country to be left
alone – they don't care what's happening in Europe as
long as this lovely place is not disturbed! They will
probably want to make peace as soon as they can,
maybe at any cost, and give Hitler all sorts of things
in return . . .

We are on ANNE. GILBERT *looks at her, worried she is*
taking him too seriously. He refills her glass.

But we needn't worry my dear, because *we'll* be staring
down at everybody from a cinema screen dressed in
ridiculous Regency dress – that's if we ever get our
call!

INT. LARGE HOUSE. AFTERNOON.
We cut to a very wide shot of ANNE *and* GILBERT *standing in*
a magnificent rococo hallway. There is a hushed silence, just a
clock ticking.

GILBERT: Where is everyone?
A young woman with long blonde hair, in a petticoat and
barefoot, walks past them giving them a radiant smile. She
disappears into the shadows of the room next door. She
leaves the door ajar. GILBERT *can't resist taking a glance*
inside. The room is in darkness; lying in the shadows on a
line of mattresses are several young women asleep in their
voluminous petticoats, their hair stretched out.

ANNE *peers over* GILBERT*'s shoulder at the young*
women and their untroubled sleep. Suddenly a voice calls.
RALPH: There you are!
They look up. RALPH *and* CELIA *are standing on the*

stairs. RALPH *is still in his dinner jacket,* CELIA *in her
petticoat as if she has just woken up.*

CELIA: You are so early! You are much too early!

ANNE: It is nearly three o'clock in the afternoon, Celia.

CELIA (*dreamily*): You missed something gorgeous . . .
There were exotic birds and fountains of gold water.

RALPH: And Aunt Elizabeth is still here! Like me she
hasn't slept all night . . .

INT. RECEPTION ROOM. AFTERNOON.

We cut to ANNE *and* GILBERT, CELIA *and* RALPH *approaching*
AUNT ELIZABETH, *who is sitting on her own in one of the
rococo reception rooms. She is at a table laid out for tea – a tea
just for her. There are little sandwiches on a silver stand and
fine china.*

ANNE: You've been up all night, Aunt Elizabeth?!

AUNT ELIZABETH: Yes, still to go to bed! I stayed up with
the young people. Haven't done that for years . . .
What amazing times we live in! I was meant to go
hours ago but I never did. (*She sees* GILBERT.) Ah,
Mr Williams, just the person I want to see!

GILBERT (*startled*): I am?

AUNT ELIZABETH: You must come here, come on –
(*indicating the chair next to her*) and hear what I've got
to tell you . . .
GILBERT *obeys her instructions.*
I've been tidying up my house, or rather the servants
have, in case we have to run like mice, and you'll
never guess what they have unearthed – my whole
collection of theatre programmes, many of them
featuring you! You in *Richard II* and the *Last Days of
Pompeii* and dozens more –

GILBERT: That is marvellous! I would love to see them.

AUNT ELIZABETH: Would you? Then you must come with
me now, because if this irritating war breaks out the
whole thing will get scattered. You don't mind coming
to my little house by St Paul's after tea?

GILBERT: No, of course not. That would be thrilling.

ANNE: Gilbert, we –

GILBERT: My career in programmes . . . ! I never kept
anything . . . I was always superstitious.

RALPH *and* CELIA *are watching the scene, amused.*

ANNE (*trying to get his attention*): Gilbert, remember we had
an appointment.

GILBERT: Oh yes, give me what you want me to listen to
dear, the record, and I will listen to it when I get
home.

ANNE *hesitates.*

I promise . . .

ANNE *quietly gives him the record.*

GILBERT: My old programmes . . . I can't resist! (*Turning
to the siblings.*) The vanity of an old actor . . .

RALPH (*grins*): I didn't say anything!

ANNE *watches* GILBERT *tuck into the sandwiches next to*
AUNT ELIZABETH.

EXT. FIELD AND GATE. DAY.
A wide shot of ANNE *standing in her Regency dress by a gate,
staring out; behind her are a field and a wood.*

*We cut to what she is staring at, and see there is a film crew
assembled in this rural location, lights blazing down; all the
crew are male except the make-up and continuity. The men are
all dressed in dark suits and ties. They are grouped round the
camera which is some distance away from* ANNE.

*There is a hush. We see everybody is looking around and
shifting from foot to foot.*

The film's DIRECTOR *is pacing furiously.*

DIRECTOR: Where is he? Where the hell is Mr Williams?

> ANNE *cranes her neck to see if she can spot any sign of him. Suddenly she sees a figure approaching down the country lane. It is* GILBERT *in his Regency costume. He is walking towards them but something in his demeanour seems strange: his face is taut and he is not hurrying.*

GILBERT: I'm late . . . I'm late . . . I'm late . . .

DIRECTOR: Why isn't the old fool running?

> GILBERT *reaches* ANNE *at the gate.*

ANNE (*concerned*): Where've you been?

> GILBERT *stares at her, his manner seems very abstracted. He doesn't reply. A make-up woman appears and starts powdering his face. The* DIRECTOR *starts shouting at them.*

DIRECTOR: We have to go straight away, I am afraid – no time for rehearsal, it is clouding over! We have to film this as soon as we can. Action!

> GILBERT *staring at* ANNE, *his manner detached.*

ANNE (*starts playing the scene*): Uncle, I know you said I shouldn't take the job at the big house but the master has been so kind to me, it is a fine opportunity.

> ANNE *can see in her peripheral vision something is causing a stir among the film crew.*

GILBERT: There will be other opportunities. I know you have your eye on him –

> ANNE *can see members of the crew turning to each other and whispering, a rustle of movement.* GILBERT *is continuing to act.*

GILBERT: But he is engaged to another, and however much you hope that situation is not going to change.

> *We are on* ANNE*'s face.*

You should listen to me, Jenny . . .

DIRECTOR: Cut! Cut! (*He stands in front of the crew.*) Excuse me . . . excuse me, everyone, I have an announcement to make . . . Apparently – I don't quite

know how to put this – we are now at war, we are at
war with Germany.

There is total silence for a moment.

Then there is a nervous shocked laugh from someone.

ANNE *immediately looks at* GILBERT. *Again he seems
very detached.*

ANNE: So it's happened . . .

DIRECTOR: Now I know the news is very shocking, but we
still have a job to do. I have asked for a wireless to be
bought here and maybe we should gather round it
when it arrives and have an early tea break . . . but for
now let's pick it up from where we were.

We are on ANNE.

DIRECTOR: Action!

ANNE *turns to continue the scene.* GILBERT *is staring at
her more directly, his tone urgent.*

GILBERT (*quietly*): Do you understand, Anne . . . ?

ANNE (*surprised, thinking she is being patronised*): Yes, I think
so – which bit do you think I don't understand, that
we're at war? Or what action means?

DIRECTOR: Come on, for God's sake! Action!

INT. THE LONDON TOWN HOUSE. NIGHT.
*It is night-time. There is a fire in the hearth in the hall in the
London town house.*

As ANNE *enters she sees that her father,* RALPH *and* CELIA
are all gathered there.

ANNE: You are not waiting for me, are you? I am sorry, it
was a very long day –

RALPH (*quiet*): We've been watching the door.

CELIA: Mama has gone to bed early . . . but we thought we
should all be together.

ALEXANDER (*with feeling*): We thought today of all days you
    might read to us?
    Time cut. ANNE *is sitting on the stairs reading a*
    Shakespeare sonnet to ALEXANDER, RALPH *and* CELIA.
    The camera moves between each of their faces as she reads.

EXT. THE YARD. THE FILM STUDIO. DAY.
ANNE *is crossing the yard at the film studio in her normal*
clothes in the early morning. In the corner of the yard the boy
messenger, MICK, *is crouching down, being sick.* ANNE *recoils*
away from him.

ANNE: For goodness' sake, Mick . . .
    We stay on MICK *after she has crossed the yard and see he*
    is shaking and looking truly shocked.

INT. THE LONG PASSAGE / COSTUME ROOM. DAY.
As soon as ANNE *enters the passage she realises something is*
very wrong. In the distance is a group of police – the police
extras we saw earlier playing football and the real police
mingled together, the plain-clothed real police telling the extras
to leave the building. We are on ANNE*'s face: all the dialogue*
from the police is off-camera, voices raised or half heard.

    As ANNE *approaches the costume room where the police are,*
we see a look of dread on her face as if she senses what she
might see.

    We are close on her as she moves through the police and into
the costume room; nobody seems to notice her for a moment.

A terrible scene greets her. GILBERT *is sitting on a chair with*
his back to her; he is surrounded by the costumes hanging up to
dry, including her Regency costume.

There is blood everywhere, part of the back of GILBERT*'s head has been blown away.*

We are close on ANNE; *she is moving in a daze further into the room, as we hear off-camera police voices talking in matter-of-fact tones. A police photographer is photographing the scene. A bluebottle is buzzing loudly on the window.*

A hand takes ANNE*'s arm and begins to steer her out of the room; a policeman's voice off-camera: 'This is not a place for you, miss . . . '*

He is guiding her out of the room, ANNE *staring around, the dazed shock on her face. She sees momentarily again, as she is being moved through the room, the appalling wound in* GILBERT*'s head, the blood on the costumes. She sees the police moving a hand gun, an old pistol, holding it carefully in a cloth.*

Again it is just a glimpse, half obscured by a policeman's back.

All around her the police are moving unhurriedly, methodically but also almost casually, as if they have already worked out what happened.

A voice says, 'We can't have people wandering into the room for goodness' sake . . . Get everybody out of this part of the building.'

ANNE *is being pushed back, past the policemen extras in uniform who are trying to stare in. The extras are appalled but fascinated. A voice is shouting, 'And get* them *out of the building too!'*

We cut to ANNE *at the end of the long passage; the costume room is now out of sight, all she can hear are voices. The boy,* MICK, *is standing with her as is the make-up woman who did* GILBERT*'s make-up in the field. The make-up woman is in deep shock and is opening and shutting her box of make-up with mechanical regularity.* MICK *indicates a cup of tea and biscuits on the window ledge.*

MICK: I was just taking him his tea, I was only a couple of
minutes late . . . He wasn't in his dressing room, that's
when I found him. They say it looks like he shot
himself . . . they said I shouldn't ask, but that's what it
looks like.

ANNE (*very quiet*): Did you see a note . . . ?

MICK: I didn't see much . . . you know . . . (*His voice trails
off, he looks very upset.*)

ANNE (*quiet*): You didn't see a note?

MICK: I couldn't really look at anything . . . (*His face
flushed, on the verge of tears.*) I was only a tiny bit late
and there he was . . . (*He looks at* ANNE, *suddenly his
voice very worried.*) And I haven't been able to get
through to them on location, I called and called, his
scene is very soon . . . It would be terrible if they were
expecting him.

INT. ANNE'S LONDON BEDROOM. AFTERNOON.
We cut to ANNE *sitting in her bedroom on the phone, a white
telephone next to her bed. The windows are shuttered. We hear
the sound of really heavy rain outside. A male voice answers at
the other end.*

MALE VOICE: Yes?

ANNE: Is that the Foreign Office?

MALE VOICE: Yes, it is.

ANNE: Can I have extension 182 please?

MALE VOICE: Hold the line a moment . . .
There is a pause. We move in on ANNE's *face; she is still
very shocked but there is a determined look in her eyes.*

FEMALE VOICE: Hello, can I help you?

ANNE: Is that extension 182?

FEMALE VOICE: Yes.

ANNE: This is Anne Keyes. Can I speak to Lawrence
    Newbolt, please?

FEMALE VOICE: Putting you through . . .

There is a pause. ANNE *looks incredibly relieved that she*
is about to hear LAWRENCE*'s voice.*

I am sorry, I made a mistake . . . I was misinformed,
Mr Newbolt is not here, he has gone to Paris.

ANNE: To Paris? But he was in Scotland . . .

FEMALE VOICE: He was in Scotland and now he is in Paris.
    He went this morning.

ANNE: This morning? How long has he gone for?

FEMALE VOICE: That is classified, of course.

ANNE: Is there a number that I can reach him on in Paris?

FEMALE VOICE: That is classified too, of course, in the
    present circumstances, I am sure you realise.

ANNE: When will you be speaking to him next?

FEMALE VOICE: I can't tell you that for the same reason.
    You will appreciate no information of that kind can
    be given out.

ANNE (*urgently*): But will it be soon?

FEMALE VOICE: One can't say, arrangements are changing
    daily –

ANNE: Will you tell him to call me urgently when you next
    speak to him whenever that is?!

FEMALE VOICE: We will. And you are Anne Lees?

ANNE: Keyes! It is very urgent, please can you tell him
    that.

FEMALE VOICE: We will pass on your message.

The phone clicks off.

The sound of rain intensifies. We move in on ANNE*'s*
face, on to her eyes.

There is a knock; her father is standing there. She is
immensely relieved to see him.

ALEXANDER: Darling, I have just seen the dreadful news in
    the evening newspaper about Mr Williams –

He moves across and takes her in his arms.
I am so sorry, you must be so upset.
He kisses her. ANNE *hugs her father really tight, holding him so close.*

ANNE: Yes . . . it's really horrible. I was very fond of him.

ALEXANDER (*stroking her hair*): What a terrible shock . . . Does anybody know what happened?

ANNE (*sitting on the edge of the bed*): They say he shot himself, that's what it looks like. But there wasn't a note. I waited for hours to see if they would find a note from him, a message. And they didn't.

ALEXANDER: He may not have written one. (*He looks across at her.*) It's an extraordinarily emotional time right now . . . for me too. War happening again . . . People react in all sorts of ways to that, there have been a lot of suicides.
He sits next to her on the bed. The sound of the rain is very loud. His voice is soft.

ALEXANDER: It seems it was so recent, the last war, and having been there myself, darling, having fought in that delightful show, I can tell you I dream about it nearly every night, see the faces of those that aren't with us now. Sometimes I wake up, I've been in the middle of a card game with them and they are all looking at me . . .

ANNE: Yes, I know . . . I know a lot of people are very confused and upset, of course I realise that. And I don't want to sound hysterical or over-dramatic –

ALEXANDER (*very fond smile*): You're an actress, some of that is required anyway –

ANNE: That's true . . .
There is a powerful sense of closeness between them, together in this austere room.

ALEXANDER (*taking her hand*): And you're so bright and original . . . full of your stories and drawings, always,

never lost that! (*Fondly.*) Your comic knights and their
adventures –

ANNE: Yes . . . (*Staring back at him forcibly.*) So I don't
want it to seem I am imagining things –

ALEXANDER: I understand.

ANNE: – and Gilbert may have killed himself after all. But
what if he didn't? What if something else is going on?
First Hector and then him –

ALEXANDER: Why would they concern themselves with
Gilbert? It isn't very likely, darling, that they are linked.

ANNE: I know . . .

ALEXANDER *holds her hand, they are very close.*

ALEXANDER: I love you.

ANNE *leans her head against him.*

Nobody knows what each day will bring at the
moment and that is very disconcerting . . . It applies
to me as well. (*He looks at her.*) One thing is certain
though – we won't allow Mr Balcombe anywhere near
us, whatever he is up to.

She looks up.

I'll keep you safe. (*He smiles.*) Some things I am still
good at, darling . . .

CELIA *comes bursting through the door into the bedroom.*

CELIA: Oh darling, I just heard the news, that's awful . . .

She puts her arms round ANNE.

EXT. THE VERANDAH. LONDON HOUSE. DAY.
*We cut to the verandah of the London house overlooking the
town garden.* MAUD *is in the garden, pruning the plants,
concentrating deeply.* RALPH, CELIA, ANNE *and* ALEXANDER
all sitting having tea, watching MAUD *garden. There are scones
and a fine collection of different jams.*

RALPH: It is amazing how much has changed in a day!

Incredible what you see – coming through the park
just now I thought I saw this huge silver beast!

CELIA: A silver beast?!

RALPH: It was in fact a barrage balloon being inflated –
but it was moving by itself along the ground! And
they say two million people are being evacuated
today! And lots and lots of people are having their
pets put down –

CELIA: Their pets? Really? How awful!

RALPH: Yes, because they are leaving town and there is
nobody to look after them, or because they feel it's
being responsible – mustn't let food be wasted on
animals . . . So that's why I have got all these jams
out, every pot we have, even the greengage! Thought
we should gorge ourselves because we might not get
another chance –

CELIA (*calling to* MAUD): Mama, you must come and have
some tea. We are eating all the jam.

MAUD: No. (*She's pruning away.*) I just want to do this.
Who knows when I'll see this garden again?

ALEXANDER (*to* ANNE): I may be going to America.

ANNE: To America?! (*Very startled.*) When are you going?

ALEXANDER: Maybe very soon – as I told you, things keep
changing. At the moment the government is suggesting
I should go there to help raise funds for the war effort
and try to get American support. (*Softly, confidentially.*)
I've got to go to some basement office tomorrow and
meet somebody I've never heard of.

ANNE *immediately looks worried on behalf of her father.
He sees her concern.*

ALEXANDER: It will be fine, darling, I am sure . . . So can
you go down to Norfolk to look after Aunt Elizabeth?
She is staying down there. You know how she hates
to be alone. Your mother will join you as soon as she
can –

MAUD: Just need to leave this garden in the best state I
    can . . .

ANNE (*worried, looking at* ALEXANDER, *concerned*): I didn't
    realise you were going away.

ALEXANDER (*softly*): Don't worry, remember what I said . . .
    It would be good if you could go to Norfolk, darling.

ANNE: Yes, I can go down there of course. They just want
    me to go back to the studio for one more day, to do
    some sound.

INT. PASSAGE. FILM STUDIO. DAY.
ANNE is approaching down the long passage in the studio.
MICK suddenly appears at the other end of the passage, calling
after her.

MICK: Oh, Miss Keyes!
    ANNE turns as MICK approaches.
    These were in your dressing room . . . I don't know if
    you meant to leave them behind.
    He hands her the gramophone record in the brown sleeve
    and a cigarette case.
    I think the cigarette case is Mr Williams's, but I didn't
    know who else to give it to.

ANNE (*taking the gramophone record*): I didn't see this in my
    dressing room when I left . . .

MICK: It was in a cupboard right at the back.

INT. DUBBING THEATRE. DAY.
We are in the darkness of a dubbing theatre. The film DIRECTOR
is sitting at the back. In the blackness, behind a glass screen, are
the technicians. We only see them as shapes in the gloom. Thick
cigarette smoke hangs in the air. ANNE *is standing at the*
microphone. There is a large cinema screen in front of her.

DIRECTOR: Now, it will be a shock seeing him again, Anne.
I know you will find it distressing, Mr Williams
springing back to life so to speak up there –

ANNE: Yes, of course it's strange, so soon after.

DIRECTOR: Yes, but I thought it best to get it out of the
way, get it done while we still can – who knows where
we will be next week?

*The film starts being projected. There on the large screen
is* GILBERT *in black and white leaning on the gate in his
Regency costume,* ANNE *next to him.*

DIRECTOR: Just need to do your first line, there was a
noise on it. (*Being encouraging.*) You look radiant up
there, Anne, don't you think?

ANNE *is staring at* GILBERT, *very moved seeing him
there, hearing his voice again.*

DIRECTOR: But Gilbert is a bit detached, isn't he, you can
see it, that he wasn't quite there. Obviously already
decided what he was going to do. Ready then?

ANNE *staring up at* GILBERT. *She attempts to lip-sync her
first line. She is trying hard not to break down.*

ANNE: Uncle, I know you said I shouldn't take the job in
the big house . . .

DIRECTOR: That was a little out, I am afraid. Maybe you
should just watch the whole scene, get in the mood.
(*He smiles.*) Perhaps we should have done that first.

The scene begins to play. ANNE *lights a cigarette, finding
it difficult to watch. The* DIRECTOR *suddenly leaps up and
yells at the screen.*

DIRECTOR: What the hell is he doing?!

ANNE *looks up, very startled.*

DIRECTOR: He is saying the wrong line, the bloody idiot.
It's utterly wrong! Rewind it . . . rewind! Got to check
that!

We see GILBERT *on the screen staring out from the gate.
His eyes meet* ANNE*'s.*

GILBERT: But he is engaged to another, and however
        much you hope that situation is not going to change,
        you should listen to it again, Anne.

DIRECTOR: Did you hear that?! 'You should listen to it
        again, Anne.' That's completely the wrong line! Rewind
        again, please.

We move in on ANNE. *She is transfixed. She is staring up
at the screen as it rewinds. The* DIRECTOR *is carrying on
in the background.*

DIRECTOR: The real line is, 'You should listen to me,
        Jenny.' He called you *Anne* instead of Jenny and
        totally rewrote the line!

We see GILBERT. *This time we are close on the screen as
he says the line, close on his mouth and then his eyes.*

GILBERT: You should listen to it again, Anne . . . (*His face
        staring down from the huge screen.*) Anne . . . listen!

ANNE *meets* GILBERT'*s gaze.*

DIRECTOR: His mind was completely elsewhere, clearly!
        I'll have to play the whole thing in close-up on you,
        Anne. Poor old bastard – 'You should listen to it
        again, Anne' – it's not even close!

We are on ANNE, *staring back at* GILBERT *on the screen.*

EXT. THE YARD. THE STUDIO. DAY.
We cut to the record in ANNE'*s hand as she comes out of the
studio building. In front of her is the Daimler with the chauffeur,*
DAWSON, *waiting for her. She slips the record into her bag as
she approaches the car.* DAWSON *moves to open the door for her
and take her bag.*

ANNE: No, that's all right, Dawson, thank you, but I'll
        keep this, I am going to read on the journey . . . It
        takes so long to get to Norfolk!

INT. THE LIMOUSINE. DAY.

We cut to ANNE *sitting on the back seat of the limousine. The bag is next to her. There is a book open on her lap and she is pretending to read it, but she can't stop herself glancing up. She looks at* DAWSON *in the driving mirror; she is twisting the cigarette case around in her hand. The sherry decanter is shaking in the drinks cabinet making a noise; she stares at it, thinking of* GILBERT.

INT. THE HOUSE IN NORFOLK. AFTERNOON.

ANNE *enters the house in Norfolk. The maid* LUCY *is in the hall,* AUNT ELIZABETH *is in the depth of field in the smaller of the two reception rooms, surrounded by tea things.*

AUNT ELIZABETH: There you are! I've been waiting to have my tea, dear, until you arrived. There's a slightly miserable-looking walnut cake . . . but the sandwiches look promising.

   ANNE *approaches* AUNT ELIZABETH *and kisses her.*

ANNE: It's been a long journey, I just need to change. (*Trying to appear relaxed.*) It looks lovely, the tea . . . *We cut to* ANNE *in the large reception room lifting the gramophone. It is a bulky machine in a cabinet and she is struggling to carry it.*

   LUCY *enters the room.*

ANNE: Oh Lucy, would you help me with this?

   LUCY *looks very surprised at* ANNE *holding the gramophone. She moves to help her.*

ANNE (*adopting a showbiz manner*): There's been a tune going round in my head all week – you know what that's like? I got a complete passion for it! And the studio has given me a copy and I simply have to listen to it right now! (*She smiles.*) I didn't want to disturb Aunt Elizabeth . . .

INT. ANNE'S NORFOLK BEDROOM. AFTERNOON.
We cut to ANNE *alone in her room. She is kneeling on the floor very close to the gramophone. The record is spinning round; she drops the needle on to it.*

MALE VOICE: So we are exploring the objectives that we
    set out and agreed upon at the last meeting and how
    we might achieve them in practice –
    The voice becomes inaudible. ANNE *lifts the needle and
    drops it later on in the record.*

MALE VOICE: – and the third objective remains, as I think
    you'll agree, as important as ever and shouldn't be
    forgotten –
    ANNE *rolls her eyes in impatience and moves the needle
    further on.*

MALE VOICE: – and I think it will simplify matters if we
    combine the next two under the same heading and
    treat them together –

ANNE (*sighs*): Oh Gilbert . . . !
    *She lifts the needle and places it right towards the end of
    the record. Immediately she hears a different voice, a voice
    she recognises.*

THE OTHER VOICE: We should make sure the scheme
    for applying the greatest possible pressure on these
    individuals is co-ordinated in one place . . .
    ANNE*'s eyes flick.*

ANNE: Balcombe . . .

BALCOMBE'S VOICE: The operation that was mounted on
    the first two individuals has been successful, as you
    are aware, and they will be troubling us no more, and
    the third one, on Hector Haldane, is I think about to
    be achieved . . . but we need – I hate to be really
    mundane – but we do now need to give this operation
    a name to ease communication amongst us, so all of
    us know instantly what we are talking about . . .

A young male voice suddenly pipes up.

YOUNG MALE VOICE: I can give you a name . . . you want
a name?

We are moving in on ANNE. *She is stunned. It is* RALPH's
voice.

RALPH'S VOICE: I've got the perfect name! Let's call it
'Thin Men Dancing' . . . !

There is muffled laughter from the men.

ANNE *is backing away from the gramophone. We hear
the men continue to chuckle on the record.* ANNE *is
surrounded by the childhood pictures of the large jousting
knights, the 'Fat Men Dancing'.*

RALPH'S VOICE: We won't forget that in a hurry! A name
like that!

BALCOMBE'S VOICE: 'Thin Men Dancing'? . . . Well, that is
certainly eccentric . . . Where does that come from?
Anyway, why not? (*He chuckles.*) No chance of
confusion there!

ANNE: Ralph . . . no . . .

ANNE *sits next to the gramophone completely frozen. The
noise of the men on the record begins to blur. We are
tracking towards* ANNE.

We see a sharp cut of RALPH *in a darkened room in the
shadows, across the table from* BALCOMBE *and a couple
of other men in dark suits.*

RALPH: I've got the perfect name! Let's call it 'Thin Men
Dancing'!

We see him through clouds of cigarette smoke, and then
BALCOMBE's *face sipping a glass of water.*

BALCOMBE: And let's see how much dancing they need
to do!

And then we see RALPH *again, his face is full of energy,
his exuberant smile.*

We cut back to ANNE, *close on her face, a massive sense
of betrayal and shock in her eyes. An abrupt cut to*

ALEXANDER's *birthday meal,* HECTOR *holding forth, his intelligent face shining out. The camera moves and we see* RALPH *watching him very carefully, a totally different angle than we have seen before.*

We cut back to ANNE's *eyes.*

Suddenly the door of the bedroom opens. LUCY *is standing there. For one moment* ANNE *can't respond; she can't move from her frozen position. She stares back up at* LUCY *blankly.* LUCY *glances at the gramophone, the male voices on the record. She looks back at* ANNE.

LUCY: I did knock, miss, I didn't think you could hear me . . .

ANNE *staring at her.*

Her Ladyship is wondering if you are ready for tea?

INT. RECEPTION ROOM. AFTERNOON.
We cut to AUNT ELIZABETH *in the reception room in the middle of her cup of tea.* ANNE *is sitting opposite her, staring at a sandwich on her plate.* AUNT ELIZABETH *is in full flow.*

AUNT ELIZABETH: Beatrice Townsend rang me yesterday and said at least there is one silver lining to this war, one won't have to wake up every Friday morning wondering if one has got the guest list right for the weekend. But I expect the competition between her and Emerald Cunard will begin again very soon, they won't let a small thing like a war stop their entertaining, nor should they, don't you agree?

ANNE (*her mind floating with the shock*): I agree it will take more than a war to stop them . . .

AUNT ELIZABETH: And we mustn't let it stop us either. We must stick together down here, my dear, or we will go absolutely mad. We will do everything together, listen to the wireless, play mahjong, go to church, do everything like twin sisters.

ANNE: Yes, Aunt Elizabeth.

She stares back at AUNT ELIZABETH, *wondering how much she knows.*

AUNT ELIZABETH: Don't look so thoughtful, my dear, I am sure we will find lots to talk about. (*She stares straight at* ANNE.) But of course you have had such a horrid shock.

ANNE'*s eyes flick.*

Poor Mr Williams, I hope it wasn't seeing his whole career spread out in those programmes from my collection that made him so desperate. Having one's life summed up can be very dispiriting! (*She sips her tea.*) This little war makes everything uncertain. (*She looks across at* ANNE.) And that's why we have to keep each other busy.

INT. ANNE'S NORFOLK BEDROOM. EVENING.

We cut to ANNE *moving round her bedroom with the record, wondering where to hide it. She slips it in among her underwear in a chest of drawers. She looks across at the pictures above the bed of the Fat Knights. Her eyes settle on one of the drawings; it is of a warrior queen brandishing a sword.* ANNE *stares at it for a moment in silence.*

INT. THE HALL, NORFOLK HOUSE. EVENING.

ANNE *is dialling on the phone in the hall,* AUNT ELIZABETH *is in the reception room in the depth of field, fast asleep. The wireless is on next to* AUNT ELIZABETH, *broadcasting an item about the RAF dropping leaflets on German cities.*

ANNE (*to the operator*): Can I have Whitehall 439, the
  Foreign Office? (*As she waits she looks across to check
  that* AUNT ELIZABETH *is still asleep.*)
MALE VOICE: The Foreign Office.
ANNE: Can I have extension 182, Lawrence Newbolt,
  please?
  *There are some curious sounds on the line, clicks, as if
  somebody is listening. Suddenly above her* ANNE *sees*
  LUCY *and another servant carrying the gramophone
  downstairs from her room.* ANNE *watches them with
  surprise.*
MALE VOICE: There is no reply from extension 182.
  ANNE *rings off. As she does so* AUNT ELIZABETH *calls
  across to her.*
AUNT ELIZABETH: You've broken the rules already my
  dear, moving the gramophone! We are going to do
  everything together, remember. I've asked them to
  bring it in here in case we want to listen to some
  music tonight. Now come in here – (*She indicates the
  wireless.*) and let's listen to what the world is getting
  up to, and if we should take it seriously . . .

EXT. NORFOLK LANDSCAPE. DAY.
A very wide shot of AUNT ELIZABETH *and* ANNE *walking
along a country road, a large sky and a landscape stretching
towards a horizon.*

AUNT ELIZABETH: I can usually only enjoy the countryside
  in very small doses . . .
  The sound of the wind, the huge empty landscape.
  But it is very peaceful here.
  ANNE *notices in the distance, at first just as a tiny dot,
  a lone cyclist coming towards them.*

AUNT ELIZABETH: The war seems such a long way off . . . although since no bombs are dropping anywhere maybe London is this quiet.

ANNE: Do you know what's happening with Papa? Have you heard from him?

AUNT ELIZABETH: No, I have not. But then he dislikes using the telephone almost as much as I do.

ANNE watching the cyclist approaching down the long straight road towards them.

ANNE: We don't seem to be alone.

AUNT ELIZABETH (*staring at the cyclist*): Anybody we know?

The cyclist is near them now. A plump man in a dark city suit and hat. He rides past them, giving them a little nod, and then continues towards the horizon.

Apparently not.

EXT. THE CHURCH. NORFOLK. DAY.
We cut to ANNE and AUNT ELIZABETH approaching the church, which is a very substantial medieval building. It is the same church they visited at night, but by day we can see it is very isolated, surrounded by empty fields.

We cut to AUNT ELIZABETH suddenly sitting down on a bench in the shadow of the church's high walls.

AUNT ELIZABETH: Just have to change my shoes, dear, after that country walk . . . You've got my other shoes, haven't you?

ANNE is carrying a small bag; she takes out AUNT ELIZABETH's other shoes.

ANNE: Let me help you . . .

AUNT ELIZABETH: Thank you, my dear.

ANNE kneels down at AUNT ELIZABETH's feet and changes her shoes. She looks up to find AUNT ELIZABETH staring down at her as if studying her closely.

AUNT ELIZABETH: I am so glad you are here to keep me
    company, my dear . . .

ANNE: Thank you.

    AUNT ELIZABETH *watches her for a moment.*

AUNT ELIZABETH: And now I am going to spoil it all and
    ask you just to scrape the shoes my dear, because if
    they go into the bag like that they will make these
    shoes all muddy when we go back. (*She leans forward.*)
    I think I saw a little scraper just round the corner . . .
    Their eyes meet. ANNE *stares right back into* AUNT
    ELIZABETH's *eyes.*

ANNE: Of course.

    We cut to ANNE *alone in the graveyard, scraping the shoes
    by the side entrance to the church. The wind is blowing,
    the vast empty landscape. She turns suddenly with a jolt,
    feeling she is being watched. The sound of the wind increases.*

    *She gets up, stares for a moment round the graveyard.
    She walks swiftly into the church.*

INT. THE CHURCH. DAY.

As ANNE *enters the church we see* AUNT ELIZABETH *and the*
VICAR *deep in conversation. They both look round very sharply
as she enters. The choirboys, including* YOUNG WALTER, *are
waiting in their blue surplices. There is nobody else in the church.*

AUNT ELIZABETH: There you are, my dear. I was just
    telling the vicar we must do some fundraising for the
    restoration – after all it was our family that built this
    church!

VICAR: And what a good job they made of it.

AUNT ELIZABETH: And hopefully we will still be looking
    after it in another thousand years!

VICAR (*to* ANNE): It must be marvellous to end up being
    part of such a family –

ANNE: To end up? I haven't just joined, you know!

VICAR: Of course. A slip of the tongue. I meant such an old-established family . . . the sense of history . . . (*He stares at her, his sharp little eyes.*) That must be such a good feeling . . .

Time cut. The choir singing an old English anthem, a rich almost ecstatic sound. The VICAR *is conducting. Only* AUNT ELIZABETH *and* ANNE *are watching.*

We move in on ANNE. *For a moment she sees a flashback of them all –* RALPH, CELIA, LAWRENCE *and* HECTOR *– moving among the ruins of the abbey, her brother leaping on to the low wall exuberantly,* HECTOR *waving his arms.*

We cut back to the choir. YOUNG WALTER *is singing but looking across at her at the same time. In the shadows* ANNE *suddenly sees the dark-suited man who was on the bicycle, sitting in a pew watching the choir. She is sure he wasn't there before. A chill goes through her. She has a powerful sense that she has got to get out of the church immediately. She glances sideways at* AUNT ELIZABETH, *who is smiling at the choir.*

For a moment ANNE *hesitates, then she suddenly convulses into a convincing coughing fit. She turns to* AUNT ELIZABETH.

ANNE: I am so sorry . . . (*Between coughs.*) I'll just get rid of this . . .

She moves down the aisle as the choir sings and YOUNG WALTER *watches.*

EXT. THE CHURCH AND COUNTRY ROAD. DAY.

We cut to ANNE *moving briskly away from the church, the sound of the choir following her. Then we cut to a very wide shot of her on the country road, walking very fast, her figure dwarfed by the sky and the view to the horizon.*

INT. THE NORFOLK HOUSE. HALL. DAY.
ANNE *enters the hall of the house; she can hear a radio, some*
light music and the voices of the servants talking, but there is
nobody in the hall. She runs upstairs.

INT. ANNE'S BEDROOM. DAY.
ANNE *grabs the record from the bottom of the drawer in her*
bedroom. She hears the footsteps of a maid passing by in the
passage. As soon as she has gone, ANNE *moves out of the room.*

EXT. OUTBUILDINGS. DAY.
ANNE *is moving towards the outbuildings. She crosses the shell*
line and runs to the second outbuilding, where she found the
keys. She starts tearing the tarpaulin off the old two-seater car
that is parked there. She can still hear the sound of the radio
from the house. She slips into the driver's seat.

ANNE: Of course it's never going to start . . .
> *She pushes the starter button and the engine kicks into life*
> *immediately. She reverses the car out, the wheels crunching*
> *over the shell line.*
>
> *She swings the car around. She can still hear the radio*
> *and laughter from the house. She starts to drive away*
> *from the outbuildings and towards where the drive of the*
> *house climbs the valley to the main gates of the estate.*
>
> *Through the windscreen she suddenly sees* LUCY
> *standing on the drive, blocking her path.* LUCY *remains*
> *stock still as the car approaches her.* ANNE *has to brake*
> *violently.*

LUCY: Miss Anne, where are you going?
ANNE: I have to go to London urgently. I got a message
    from work.
LUCY: That car is not safe to drive, Miss Anne.
ANNE: I've got to go, Lucy!
> ANNE *puts her foot down and veers off the drive and on*

to the grass to avoid running LUCY *over. The car bobbles along across the grass for a moment, failing to pick up speed.* LUCY *is running after her calling and calling.*

LUCY: Miss Anne, don't go! Miss Anne, *don't go!*
The car manages to pick up speed. ANNE *can see* LUCY *in the mirror, a receding figure but still calling her name again and again.*

EXT. LONG STRAIGHT ROAD. DAY.
We cut to a wide shot of the car travelling down a long straight road. We see a close-up of ANNE *glancing at the speedometer; she changes gear.*

ANNE: You're not going to give out on me . . . !
Very loud engine noise. She stares in the driving mirror; the road behind her is totally empty. Through the windscreen there is also just a completely empty road. She stares ahead.
Where is everybody?
She glances sideways at the passing countryside, the huge empty vistas.
   Suddenly coming over the brow of the hill in front of her is a large truck covered in tarpaulin and belching exhaust fumes. It roars past her in a cloud of smoke and noise. And then ANNE *sees in the driving mirror that the truck has slowed and then completely stopped.*
   She goes round the corner and loses sight of the truck. But a moment later it comes up behind her in the driving mirror and starts to bear down on her.

ANNE (*alarmed*): What the hell does he want?
The truck is right behind her. She slows and it draws level with her, still belching smoke. She can't see into the driver's cabin. She slows even more to allow it to get away.
   It disappears over the horizon, its engine noise echoing over the empty landscape after it has gone.

There is relief in ANNE*'s face. She speeds up, the road stretches ahead of her.*

She goes round a corner. In front of her about a hundred yards away is a military road block manned by three military policemen. There is no sign of the truck.

ANNE *drives up to the road block and stops. One of the military policemen approaches the car; he is a large man with a very officious manner.*

MILITARY POLICEMAN: The road ahead is closed, there is a military exercise taking place. You will have to find another route through.

ANNE *looks at the road stretching ahead.*

ANNE: I am going to London . . .

The MILITARY POLICEMAN *just staring at her.*

So how do I get there?

MILITARY POLICEMAN: By another route.

ANNE (*sharp*): Thank you for that, just thought you might be able to help. And where is the lorry that passed me? You seem to have allowed him through with no problem!

The MILITARY POLICEMAN *stares at her with very sharp, officious eyes. He takes exception to her tone.*

MILITARY POLICEMAN: Could you switch off your engine, please.

ANNE *hesitates and then does so.*

MILITARY POLICEMAN: Can I see your identity card?

ANNE: My identity card? I don't have one.

MILITARY POLICEMAN: You don't have one? From yesterday everybody has to carry an identity card, miss. It is the law. There are no exceptions. I am afraid I will have to detain you.

ANNE (*very alarmed*): Detain me? Why? I've been down here in the country, I came straight here from the film studio, that's why I haven't got one! I really must get to London today –

MILITARY POLICEMAN: If you don't have a card you're not
    going anywhere.

ANNE: I am the daughter of a member of parliament, Sir
    Alexander Keyes, I am sure if you telephone him, or
    let me –

MILITARY POLICEMAN (*very sharp*): Step out of the
    vehicle, please.

ANNE hesitates for a second. She gets out of the car.

*A wide shot of the isolated road, the road block, the big
sky dwarfing them.*

Move over to that side of the vehicle, please . . .

ANNE reluctantly moves to the other side of the car.

Get into the vehicle . . . !

*One of the other military policemen gets into the driving
seat of the car and switches on the engine.*

ANNE: Where are we going?

*The policeman who is driving is totally expressionless. The
car moves off, through the road block and on. The road in
front of them stretches ahead on to the horizon.*

   *ANNE glances back at the receding road block and then
at the driver.*

Where are you taking me?

The driver doesn't even acknowledge her.

I think you might at least tell me where I am going?!

INT. VILLAGE HALL. DAY.

*We cut to a wide shot of a village hall with whitewashed rustic
walls and long wooden benches. ANNE is sitting on one of the
wooden benches. The only door to the hall is open, but a soldier
is guarding the exit. He is standing with his back to ANNE, but
frequently glancing in her direction with a sexual gaze. Behind
ANNE, sitting on another wooden bench, are an elderly married
couple, who are looking very nervous.*

A loud clock is ticking. Suddenly another soldier in uniform enters and addresses the elderly couple with a sharp tone.

SOLDIER IN UNIFORM: So if I can ask you to come this
way now . . .
The couple look round anxiously but do not move. The soldier's tone becomes more aggressive.
SOLDIER IN UNIFORM: Come on quickly! . . . We have had
a lot of people like you today taking no notice of the
regulations and this is what happens!
The couple shuffle off out of the hall escorted by the
SOLDIER. *They disappear down a long passage.* ANNE *is now completely alone except for the other soldier, who is still watching her.*

The MILITARY POLICEMAN *who questioned her at the road block suddenly appears from outside. He has a plate with him and a mug of tea. On the plate is a large sandwich. He sits a few benches away from* ANNE *and starts eating his sandwich and sipping his tea. The hall is filled with the noise of him eating.* ANNE *is increasingly tense.*

ANNE: Hello again . . .
The MILITARY POLICEMAN *goes on eating.*
I don't suppose you are going to tell me how long
I am going to be held here?
MILITARY POLICEMAN (*chewing loudly*): I wouldn't complain
if I were you, miss . . . We have the power now to
detain anybody indefinitely, did you know that?
ANNE: I didn't know that, no.
MILITARY POLICEMAN: Habeas corpus . . . (*He chews
loudly.*) Do you know what 'habeas corpus' is, miss?
ANNE: Of course. Of course I do.
MILITARY POLICEMAN: Well, it doesn't exist any more, it's
gone! We can keep you as long as we want, wherever
we want . . . (*He goes on chewing.*) Don't need to ask a
judge any more, don't need to ask anybody . . . (*He*

chews, removes a bit of gristle from his teeth and puts it on his plate.) Don't even need to tell anybody where you've gone.

ANNE *suddenly really angry at this complacent threat.*

ANNE: Yes, but the press are still there, aren't they! They can write about it!

The MILITARY POLICEMAN *looks up, surprised at this.*

MILITARY POLICEMAN: That is true . . . (*He chews.*) For the moment.

ANNE: And if you start throwing people into jail for no reason they bloody well will be writing about it . . .

The MILITARY POLICEMAN *lights a cigarette.*

ANNE (*deciding to be placatory*): I wasn't complaining just now – well I suppose I was! – but I know you have a job to do, of course I realise that.

The MILITARY POLICEMAN'*s eyes flick.*

And I am very sorry I didn't have my identity card, I should have had. But I just need to get to London . . .

The MILITARY POLICEMAN *stares across at her, his tone casually menacing.*

MILITARY POLICEMAN: Oh I assure you – you will get to London.

Time cut. High shot of the hall. The sun is setting, streaking the white walls.

ANNE *is stretched out on the wooden bench, totally alone in the hall.*

Suddenly she hears laughter and voices from outside.

RALPH *and* CELIA *appear in the doorway, framed against the light.*

RALPH: Glorious, what are you doing? What has happened to you?

ANNE *for a second reveals her disquiet at seeing* RALPH. *But he is right across the hall, and as he and* CELIA *approach,* ANNE *adopts a radiant smile as if incredibly relived to see them.*

ANNE: Thank God you're here!

CELIA: Yes, Papa got a call from these soldiers or police or whoever they are saying you had been detained! They phoned the Houses of Parliament!

RALPH: And Aunt Elizabeth telephoned to say you had just rushed out coughing like you were going to die in the middle of choir practice . . .

He smiles, staring down at her.

The vicar was heartbroken apparently!

He sits opposite her.

Why did you do that, Glorious?

ANNE: Because I had to get away . . .

She stares back at RALPH *and* CELIA. *There is a pause.*

I have a bit of a confession to make . . . I am sure it won't come as a great surprise.

She meets RALPH*'s gaze.*

I am terribly in love, I am so in love with Lawrence . . . I just can't bear being away from him, shut away in the country like that! I was filled with this incredible urge to see him.

CELIA*'s eyes are shining*

I just have to find him . . .

CELIA*'s reaction is spontaneous and heartfelt.*

CELIA: How wonderful, darling! That is fantastic!

RALPH (*smiles*): That's pretty romantic, Glorious, yes.

CELIA: And we've got news, there is a party tonight at the Foreign Office – and we sort of helped arrange it – and Lawrence is going to be there! (*She beams.*) Isn't that good timing?

ANNE (*trying not to seem too anxious*): Is he?

CELIA: And now you have been detained you've got to come too!

RALPH (*smiles*): Nothing can stop the parties happening, despite a little thing like war breaking out – especially not this one, as you will see – it's all the ambassadors!

CELIA (*kissing her*): We've got to get you ready! Got to
make you look amazing . . .

EXT. LONG STRAIGHT ROAD. OUTSIDE HALL. LATE
AFTERNOON.
As ANNE *comes out of the hall she is greeted by the sight of two
vehicles, her car and the Daimler.* DAWSON *is standing in his
chauffeur's uniform by the Daimler, staring at her impassively.
The* MILITARY POLICEMAN *is smoking in the doorway,
watching her go.*

RALPH: Dawson will drive your car back to Aunt Elizabeth.
ANNE (*sharply*): I thought it was dangerous to drive?
RALPH: Apparently it is! That's why you shouldn't have
been driving it. (*Charming smile.*) But Dawson is
expendable, isn't he! (*Teasing smile to* DAWSON.) Lots
more where you came from, aren't there! (*He moves.*)
And I get to drive the Daimler for once, which is
terrific. (*He opens the car door.*) Come on, Glorious . . .
we're hosts to today's party, remember – lots to do!
CELIA (*warm smile*): Yes, including a hot bath for you,
darling, because you look a real country girl like that!

INT. LONDON HOUSE. BATHROOM / PASSAGE. NIGHT.
We cut to ANNE *approaching along a passage towards a
bathroom full of steam. She is still dressed in her clothes from
the country.* CELIA *is standing in the bathroom waiting for her,
holding some fresh towels carefully folded.*

CELIA: A lovely hot bath, darling! You've time to have a
real good wallow before you see him . . .
ANNE *moves into the bathroom.*
The steam fills the screen.

INT. ANNE'S BEDROOM. LONDON HOUSE. NIGHT.
We cut to ANNE *and* CELIA *in* ANNE*'s bedroom. They are
wearing their dresses for the party.* CELIA *is in an exquisite
silver dress.* ANNE *is in dark red. The white cat, Horatio, is on
the bed.*

CELIA (*staring at* ANNE *in the mirror*): I think that's the one,
     I am *sure* that's the one, you've got to wear it! (*She
     picks up the white cat.*) You see Horatio agrees with me.
ANNE (*quietly staring into the mirror*): If you say so . . . I'll
     do what I am told.
CELIA (*suddenly*): Well, that would be the first time ever,
     wouldn't it?!
     ANNE *turns in surprise.*
     Always done what you wanted and told us what to
     do . . .
ANNE (*really startled, a pause*): Is that what you think?
CELIA: Only joking, darling! (*She turns.*) And anyway,
     actresses have to do what they want, don't they . . . to
     be creative!
     She moves close to ANNE.
     He'll fight duels over you with you looking like that
     if anybody tries to take you away. Lawrence will look
     after you . . .

INT. LONDON HOUSE. RECEPTION ROOM. NIGHT.
*We cut to a wide shot of the reception room in the London
house. All the furniture and dust sheets have gone.* ANNE *is
holding the white cat Horatio.*

CELIA: You see, everything has gone now, it's in storage,
     and with the whole town blacked out, isn't it strange,
     darling?! It's like being in another place completely,
     on the moon or something!

ANNE *staring across at her sister in her silver dress.*

ANNE: You look so lovely.

CELIA (*putting on a Scarlett O'Hara voice*): Why, thank you.
  (*She moves.*) I am the hostess of this party in a way,
  so I am just a tiny bit nervous, it's part of my new job,
  I am attached to the court of St James now! So I am
  going to need to go a little early –

RALPH *is in the doorway in his dinner jacket.*

RALPH: That's fine, I will escort Anne. We'll go together.

ANNE (*looking across at her brother*): Right . . . (*She turns.*)
  I must volunteer too – I've got to do something for
  the war effort.

RALPH: No, Glorious, you don't have to do that. You're an
  actress. That's what you keep doing.

CELIA: Ah, but talking of volunteering –

INT. BASEMENT PASSAGE. LONDON HOUSE. NIGHT.
We cut to ANNE *and* CELIA *moving along a basement passage
in their party dresses, past a dolls' house and piles of boxes.*

CELIA: A lot of our childhood things down here . . . not
  sure what's going to happen to them.

At the end of the passage is a travelling cage with a cat in it.

CELIA: Do you recognise him? It's Bombardier.

ANNE: Oh yes, of course, Aunt Elizabeth's cat.

CELIA (*suddenly turning*): So, darling, this is a little bit
  nasty, but Aunt Elizabeth wants him put down because
  she's shut up her house and left London, and I was
  going to have to take him to the vet, but now you're
  here could you do it?

ANNE *looking at* CELIA, *stunned.*

I'm needed at work, you see, and I can't ask one of
  the servants to do it and I would get so upset taking
  him anyway! Will you do it?

ANNE: Does Aunt Elizabeth really want that to happen?

CELIA: Yes, it has to be done, it's what people are doing!
There's nobody to look after him, and we mustn't
waste food apparently. *Please* say you'll do it!

ANNE (*quiet, staring at her*): If it has to be done . . .

INT. STAIRCASE / PASSAGE. THE FOREIGN OFFICE. NIGHT.
We see ANNE *and* RALPH *going up a grand marble staircase;*
ahead of them is a long passage stretching towards a room full
of light. The staircase and the passage are extremely dark.
RALPH *watches* ANNE *go up the staircase ahead of him in her*
dark red dress.

RALPH: You look so good, Glorious . . .

> ANNE *stops at the top and stares down at her brother. He*
> *appears so handsome and charming in his dinner jacket,*
> *for a moment it doesn't seem possible to her that he is*
> *involved.*
>
> *They start to move down the passage towards the light.*
> *They can see various figures in evening dress casting*
> *shadows on the wall and the sound of polite laughter.*
>
> CELIA *sees* ANNE *and* RALPH *approach and comes out*
> *of the room to meet them.*

CELIA: Here you are . . . So far no disasters!

RALPH: You mean they haven't started throwing things yet.
Give them time!

CELIA (*glancing back into the room*): Argentina has been
extremely talkative . . . and of course America, Mr
Kennedy, he keeps going on about how much stronger
Germany is than we are and how everything is over
for us and we better realise it! And I'm worried France
will think the wine is rather inferior . . . so fingers
crossed! (*She turns to* ANNE.) But, darling, you must

go downstairs to the other party . . . that's altogether
more fun. Papa is waiting for you there – and you
know who of course!

ANNE (*hesitates*): Downstairs?

RALPH: I'll take you . . . it's a little difficult to find.

INT. BASEMENT ROOMS AND PASSAGES. NIGHT.

RALPH *and* ANNE *moving through the dark basement passages;*
they are claustrophobic and sinister, but ahead ANNE *can hear*
the sound of children's voices and as they get nearer the passage
is full of balloons.

They enter a long basement room lined with a large map of
the world, but it is also full of more balloons and party
streamers and a group of children between the ages of seven and
fifteen, who are being given a party. In the middle of them all is
ALEXANDER *in a dinner jacket, looking very suave and clearly*
charming the pale-faced children.

ALEXANDER: Now I have a series of flags here, these little
flags . . . (*He holds out a handful of large drawing pins*
with blue flags attached.) Somewhere on the map of the
world over there is some treasure . . . so you stick
your flag in where you think the treasure is . . . and
whoever is the nearest will get a rather marvellous
prize! So come on, everybody, take a flag and – wait
for it – there is also a prize for the person who's
furthest from the treasure! (*He grins.*) That's the sort
of prize I used to win when I was little –

The children are crowding round to get their flags.

ALEXANDER *sees* ANNE.

Darling! There you are . . .

ALEXANDER *moves towards her, kisses her, the children*
following to get their flags.

It's terrific to see you.

ANNE (*embracing her father*): You're not angry with me? For
    leaving Norfolk?

ALEXANDER (*softly*): Of course not, I understand . . . (*He
    turns to* RALPH.) You take over and organise the
    treasure hunt . . . Children, Ralph here will now be
    in charge!

RALPH: Gladly, just don't forget to tell me where the
    treasure really is.

The children mill round RALPH; *some are already pinning
    their blue flags into the map of the world. Their pale faces
    looking eager for attention and warmth.*

ALEXANDER: It's all the children of the ambassadors in
    London . . . poor things . . . Lots of them don't know
    whether they are going to be travelling back to their
    countries or not. They just don't know what's
    happening –

ANNE: A bit like us then?

ALEXANDER: A bit like us . . . yes . . .

He takes her hand.

I should never have sent you to the country with Aunt
    Elizabeth . . . how could I have done that?

He holds her tight.

You belong here . . . with all of us. (*Looking down at
    her.*) I mustn't let you go away again.

ANNE: So you're not going to America then?

ALEXANDER: Not quite yet, no . . .

ANNE *can see out of the corner of her eye* RALPH *watching
    her. Her father whispers.*

ALEXANDER: Now you must go and get yourself some
    jelly . . .

ANNE (*laughs*): Some jelly? Why?

ALEXANDER (*softly, confidentially*): You should go and get
    yourself some strawberry jelly . . .

ANNE *goes into the second basement room, where two
    children are sitting rather sorrowfully eating jelly. Sitting*

by a table which is covered by different flavoured jellies
and holding a blue flag is LAWRENCE.

ANNE: Lawrence!

She moves to him. He puts his arms around her.

I didn't know whether you would really be here!

LAWRENCE: Darling . . . (*He kisses her.*)

ANNE: And I didn't know whether I would ever see you
again . . .

LAWRENCE: Yes, they suddenly sent me to France . . .

The sound of the children from the other room is very
loud. ANNE *is fighting back tears.*

Don't cry . . .

ANNE (*determinedly*): I am not going to cry. It's just it seems
for a moment everything is all right, but I know it
really isn't.

We cut back to ALEXANDER *in the main room with*
RALPH *and the children.*

ALEXANDER: When we've all got our flags pinned up . . .
I think we will have a little bit of a sing-song – a song
from each of your countries. Does everybody like the
sound of that?

We cut back to LAWRENCE *and* ANNE. *They are in the*
furthest corner of the second room; they can't be seen from
the first room but they can hear the children loudly. They
are very close, in each other's arms.

ANNE: Something terrible is going on . . .

LAWRENCE: I know.

ANNE: Ralph is involved.

LAWRENCE: I know that too.

ANNE: You know? Do you think he realises the full extent
of what they're doing? Maybe he doesn't?

LAWRENCE: I don't know the answer to that –

ANNE (*softly*): My brother . . . I can't believe he would –
(*She stops. Intense, quiet.*) I want to believe he couldn't.

LAWRENCE: What I have found out is there's a group of

them in the Secret Service, and a motley collection of
other people – some very determined aristocrats –
who are trying to bring this war to an end before it's
even started . . . They think we haven't got a chance
and they are determined to do a deal with Hitler.

ANNE: I think they killed my friend Gilbert . . . and they
blackmailed Hector . . .

LAWRENCE: They are dangerous, yes. Some powerful
people . . .

*The children's singing starts next door, at first a French
song.*

ANNE: They drove Hector to kill himself, I've got a
recording of a meeting -

LAWRENCE: Give it to me . . .

ANNE: I haven't got it here!

LAWRENCE: I really need to have that, to have proof is very
important . . . I must get it tomorrow.

Their lips are very close.

We must meet in the morning . . . but somewhere
I am not being watched, which isn't easy, it can't be
a government building and it can't be one of our
homes –

ANNE: I know – at the vet's!

LAWRENCE: The vet's?! (*He laughs.*)

ANNE: Yes, I've got to take a cat to be put down tomorrow.
We could meet there?

LAWRENCE: That sounds rather perfect –

RALPH *suddenly comes into the room.* ANNE *sees him out of
the corner of her eye. She starts to really kiss* LAWRENCE.

ANNE (*whispering between kisses*): It's all right, we're in love.

LAWRENCE (*smiles, softly*): Are we?

ANNE: That's what I told them and now that's what they're
going to see.

She kisses him passionately, her body pressed close.

Oh Lawrence . . .

RALPH (*picking up some jelly, calling across*): Not in front of
    the children, Glorious!
    He steers the two children next door.
      *We cut back into the main room. The children are now
    singing along in English; their worried, pale faces.* CELIA
    comes into the room beaming and smoking a cigarette.
ALEXANDER: This is the easy one – this is the American
    song.
    We cut back to ANNE *and* LAWRENCE, *their bodies close
    in the shadows; she kisses him again.*
ANNE: I wish I could have talked to you sooner . . .
LAWRENCE: I know . . . I am here now . . . (*He holds her
    tight.*) If we are going to use your idea, I'd better get
    the address of a vet, because we mustn't go to one
    near your house – we need one out of the way, in the
    suburbs –
ANNE: Right.
LAWRENCE: I'll do it now – use the great resources of this
    building.
ANNE (*holding him close*): *Don't go.*
LAWRENCE: I won't be a moment.
    *He disappears down the passage. One of the children is
    singing a song in Greek from next door, his little piping
    voice ringing out.* CELIA *is now supervising the singing.*
    ALEXANDER *is standing in the doorway, looking across
    at* ANNE.
ALEXANDER: Now we've started the singing, we will have
    to do every single country! (*He smiles.*) Not my most
    brilliant idea.
RALPH (*suddenly coming back into the room*): Come with me,
    Glorious, I've got something to show you.
ANNE: Come with you where?
RALPH: Follow me, it's important. (*Turns to his father.*)
    I think you should come as well . . .

INT. SUBTERRANEAN PASSAGES. NIGHT.
We are moving with RALPH, ALEXANDER *and* ANNE *along the subterranean passages.* ANNE *is moving reluctantly, she keeps stopping, but* RALPH *is moving them along. The sound of children singing is getting fainter and fainter.*

ANNE: It's such a big basement . . . Where are we going?

RALPH: You've only seen a corner of it.

ALEXANDER: More and more work is being done
    underground now.
    Now they can no longer hear the singing. RALPH *stops by a door and pushes it open. He reveals a small office and a single desk. At the desk is a woman typing; a file lies next to her.* ANNE *hesitates by the door.*

RALPH: Come on in . . . This is Miss Semel.

ANNE: She's working late.

RALPH: She is . . . and Miss Semel has two things for you,
    Anne.
    He picks something up from the desk.
    Your identity card!

ANNE: That was quick . . .

ALEXANDER: Splendid . . . I asked Ralph to arrange it and
    that *is* quick. Rather a long walk to get to it though!
    So that's perfect . . . you have your card now – you
    are officially you! (*He smiles.*) I'd better get back to
    the ambassadors, darling, I've spent rather too much
    of this party with the children, they are so much more
    interesting! (*He moves off.*)

ANNE: I'll come with you –

RALPH: Just a moment.

ANNE (*turning in the door*): What is it?

RALPH: Why are you running away, Glorious?

ANNE: I wasn't running away. Why would I do that?

RALPH: I don't know. I found out the other thing, the one

we talked about. It seems a rather appropriate moment
to do it, to go with your card . . . if you want.

ANNE: What, you mean about my parents?

RALPH: Want to hear, or do you want to run off?

RALPH is looking straight at her, as if testing her. ANNE
hesitates, stares back at him.

ANNE: OK, why not?

MISS SEMEL, *without being prompted, gets up with her
handbag and leaves the office.*

RALPH: Good night, Miss Semel.

He stares at ANNE. *He seems to want to show off to her,
to control her.*

Are you sure?

ANNE (*meeting his gaze*): I said why not.

RALPH: I think you'll be pleased. It explains your theatrical
bent – well, I think it does! They were a Romany
family . . . your parents were gypsies.

He opens the file and hands it to her.

There are no pictures sadly.

As she looks at the document.

One of them must have been blonde, mustn't they?
Maybe they had Russian blood.

ANNE *stares for a moment at the document. She closes it
and gives it back.*

ANNE: Thank you. I like the idea, you're right. I see
nothing wrong in coming from gypsies. (*She stares at
her brother.*) I am going to get back to the party now.

We cut to ANNE *moving down the dark subterranean
passage. She can hear singing some way in the distance.
She is desperate to find* LAWRENCE. *She looks over her
shoulder to see if* RALPH *is following her, but she is alone.
She turns a corner in the passage; the singing is louder but
still some distance off. She hears a noise and stops. She
can see a shadow at the end of the passage.*

ANNE: Lawrence . . . ? (*She moves closer.*) Hello? Who's
that . . . ?

*There is a sound in the darkness. She still can't see who it
is. The figure moves and disappears.* ANNE *continues down
the passage and round the corner.*

She sees the figure again moving in the darkness.

ANNE: Who's that?!

The figure turns. She gets closer.

It is the boy, WALTER.

ANNE: Walter?! How can you be here? You were in the
church this morning!

YOUNG WALTER: You're here and you were in the church.

ANNE: Why are you here? I didn't realise you were the son
of an ambassador.

YOUNG WALTER (*his solemn eyes staring back*): They thought
I might be able to contribute to the party.

ANNE: And I am sure you will be . . . Excuse me.

*She walks past him and continues down the passage. The
children's singing is much louder.* YOUNG WALTER *calls
after her.*

YOUNG WALTER: Anne . . . (*She turns to look at him.*) Don't
you realise . . .

ANNE: Don't I realise what?

The singing is louder. YOUNG WALTER *stares at* ANNE *for
a moment and then he mouths.*

YOUNG WALTER: They don't love you . . .

ANNE *stares at the boy transfixed. He mouths again.*

They don't love you.

ANNE *is genuinely frightened. She turns and walks fast
down the passage and away from the boy. She turns a
corner and walks straight into* LAWRENCE.

ANNE: Oh Lawrence! Thank God it is you.

She puts her arms round him and holds on to him tight.

LAWRENCE: What is this? I wasn't that long! . . . And I

have an address for you . . . (*He smiles.*) You see, you
can find out anything here –

ANNE: Yes – I've just discovered that . . . (*She takes the
address.*)

LAWRENCE: We'll meet there. Put the evidence you've got
in an envelope, but address it to someone other than
me –

ANNE: Right. Who?

LAWRENCE: Anybody . . . (*He smiles.*) Winston Churchill –

ANNE: Right . . . I think they are watching me as well
now . . . Will they follow me there?

LAWRENCE: No – keep an eye out, but I don't think so . . .
They won't follow you into the vet anyway.
He smiles and kisses her.
They are too squeamish.

EXT. TERRACE AND GARDEN. LONDON HOUSE. DAY.
Morning light. ANNE *appears on the terrace holding the
travelling cage with Bombardier in it.* ALEXANDER *is working
at a table in the garden, official papers all around him.*
He looks up.

ALEXANDER: There you are, darling . . .

ANNE: Yes, I am off now to take Bombardier to the vet
for – well you know what for . . .

ALEXANDER: Yes, what things have come to . . . I'm being
engulfed in paperwork now I am dealing with the
ambassadors. They keep writing to me with loads of
requests –

ANNE: Well, I am sure they all had a good party last night.
(*She starts to move off.*) There may be a lot of people at
the vet so I could be gone a little while . . .

ALEXANDER: By the way, Anne, if this is not too much to

ask, I think you'd better take Horatio too – he needs
to be done as well.

ANNE (*stunned*): Horatio . . . take our cat? Why?

ALEXANDER: Because if I am going to the US next week
we will be shutting up the house – and he can't be
sent down to the country, he will fight with the other
cats. You know what he is like . . .

ANNE: I can't take Horatio to be put down . . . I can't do
that.

ALEXANDER: No, it's too much to ask, you're right. Of
course it's very upsetting, I do realise. I hate the idea
myself. We will get Dawson to take both of them
tomorrow. He is too busy today – you don't need to
go at all, darling, Dawson will see to it. Instead you
can come and help me with these papers.

ANNE *is standing with the cat in its cage. She is trying to
think quickly.*

ANNE: I'll take Bombardier because Aunt Elizabeth has
asked for that to happen, but we will find another
home for Horatio. I am sure I can –

ALEXANDER: No, darling, we can't do that. I need to set an
example because of my position. A lot of other people
are having to do this . . .

ANNE (*suddenly*): But why are they? Surely they can be told
it's not necessary yet, because it isn't!

ALEXANDER: I find myself having to tell them it is. Anyway,
I will get Dawson to do it all, don't worry yourself.
Come and sit down and help me, I need your help.

Close-up of ANNE. *For a moment she can't think what to
do. She stares down at* ALEXANDER. *Then she makes a
decision.*

ANNE: No, I am the only one not doing anything at the
moment. So I should do it, if that's what's required.
I will take the cats to be put to sleep. Then I'll help
you.

INT./EXT. THE TAXI. DAY.

*ANNE is sitting in the back of the taxi with the two cats in
separate cages. The taxi is driving through an open area such as
Wimbledon Common on the edge of London. We see everything
from inside the taxi. The cats are staring out of their cages.
ANNE glances at the brown envelope with the record inside; it is
addressed to Winston Churchill. Then she glances out of the
window. She sees a couple of children running along a path and
then a bonfire burning, thick black smoke. A shot of another
child staring at her from the common, and then another, smaller
bonfire.*

ANNE (*to the cats*): There's no school any more, they've
    shut them, and yet they haven't evacuated these
    children . . . so they're running wild.
    The white cat looking back at her.
    Forgive me, Horatio . . . in fact both of you forgive
    me. We will meet Lawrence, but I am not going to let
    them do anything to you . . . I will find a way.

EXT./INT. VETERINARY SURGERY. DAY.

*We cut to a short queue of mostly middle-aged people with their
pets: dogs and cats and a rabbit. The VET's surgery is a red
brick building with a stable block on the edge of the common.
ANNE is moving along the queue, seeing if she can find
LAWRENCE. She gets to the front door, which is open, and
peers in. She can't see LAWRENCE inside. As ANNE stands in
the doorway, a young woman, MISS CROWLEY, with a sharp
manner addresses her from her desk in the lobby.*

MISS CROWLEY: Have you filled out your form?
ANNE: My form? What form? No, I have just arrived.
MISS CROWLEY: Have you come here to have your pets
    put down?

ANNE (*hesitates*): Yes, but I am meeting someone first, I am
　　just looking to see –

MISS CROWLEY: You can't join the queue until you have
　　filled out the consent form. All these people have filled
　　out their forms. You must come inside and fill out your
　　form.

INT. THE LOBBY. THE VET'S. DAY.
ANNE *is sitting in the lobby of the* VET'*s, slowly filling out her
form.* MISS CROWLEY *is at her desk with a mound of consent
forms in front of her. There is a small dog chained to the wall.
The queue is outside, some very distressed faces.* ANNE *can see
the smoke from the bonfires hanging over the common.*

　　ANNE *stares about her looking for* LAWRENCE. *The cats'
faces peering out of the cages uncomprehendingly at what is
happening.*

　　The door of the surgery opens, but it is the VET, *a tall,
powerful man with twinkling eyes. The* VET *nods at* ANNE *and
moves over to* MISS CROWLEY.

THE VET: We will be closing early today, Miss Crowley, as
　　we are running low on supplies . . .
　　The VET *checks the list on the desk, looks at* ANNE *again
　　and then disappears back into his surgery.* ANNE *goes up
　　to the desk with her form.*

ANNE: I haven't quite finished filling it out, I haven't
　　signed it, because I am merely –

MISS CROWLEY (*suddenly reaches up and takes the form*):
　　That will do. Not everybody signs them. As long as it
　　is filled out. It's not the law, you know, that people
　　have to do this to their pets. They're doing it because
　　they are leaving London or because they feel it is the
　　responsible thing to do. But we don't want to make any
　　mistakes, do we? Now we do have tea and biscuits –

(*reading her name off the form*) Miss Keyes . . . but
there *is* an extra charge for that, you will appreciate it
is because we are so busy.

ANNE: No, thank you. I won't have the tea. Has anybody
been asking for me? I was meeting a friend here, until
then I'm not –

The door of the VET*'s surgery opens at that moment and
a woman comes out looking very distressed. The* VET*'s face
looks round the door.*

THE VET: You may come in . . . (*he glances at* MISS CROWLEY
for ANNE*'s name*) . . . Miss Keyes.

ANNE: But I haven't been in the queue yet – I don't want
to queue-jump, I have just been doing the form . . .

THE VET (*his voice insistent*): Please come in here, Miss
Keyes. And bring your cats, of course . . .

INT. SURGERY. DAY.

We cut to ANNE *entering the surgery. She puts the cats down in
a corner. There are a series of syringes lying in little bowls in a
line on the table. Otherwise the room is very bare and spotless.
The* VET *is washing his hands; he starts speaking with his back
to her.* ANNE *very conscious of the row of syringes.*

THE VET: We're being inundated at the moment, I think
because we have the space to deal with large animals
as well which of course you don't get in the centre of
town! (*He turns to look at her.*) We've had to put down
several horses in the last few days, a donkey, I don't
know what's going to come through the door next . . .
or in the case of the big ones up to the window, to be
more accurate. But it is amazing how quickly one
becomes used to such things . . .

ANNE: I see . . . I really feel I shouldn't jump the queue.
Why am I jumping the queue?

THE VET: You seemed to us to be a little agitated.

ANNE: I am not agitated. There are people crying out
there – I think I am quite calm in comparison.

THE VET: We like people to be certain about what they are
doing and you seem to be rather upset and nervous.
(*He stares straight at her.*) Believe me, I can tell . . .

ANNE: Well, maybe I need a little time just to sit and
consider, until I meet my friend I won't be ready –

THE VET: I thought so . . . we have set aside a little room –
it's just through here – precisely for this purpose . . .
for people to make sure.

ANNE *hesitates.*

It's best you use it.

We cut to ANNE *in the little room sitting with the two cats.
They stare back at her from their cages. There is a window
in the little room overlooking the outbuildings, which are
congregated around a courtyard. There is a clock ticking.*
ANNE *is getting increasingly worried that there is no sign
of* LAWRENCE. *She starts to pace. She can hear* MISS
CROWLEY *talking to somebody in the lobby.*

MISS CROWLEY: The tea is extra, as I said, but some
people like to sit for a little while afterwards . . .
Everybody has their own different way of coping.

Suddenly through the window ANNE *sees lying on the
ground near an outbuilding one of the blue flags from the
treasure hunt at the party. She opens the door and begins
to cross the yard towards the outbuilding. She can hear*
MISS CROWLEY'*s voice continuing to talk to the queue.*

MISS CROWLEY: Please make sure you say goodbye before
you go into the surgery, it's much the best way of
doing things.

MISS CROWLEY'*s voice grows fainter.*

ANNE *reaches the outbuilding; she pushes the door open.*

INT. OUTBUILDING. DAY.

She is greeted by the eerie sight of a long line of what look like brown-paper parcels hanging from hooks stretching out into the darkness. She walks through the parcels, knocking into one of them and sees the head of a dead dog protruding out of the bottom. She realises she is standing in a room completely full of animal corpses.

A terrible chill goes through her, but she can see a door ajar ahead of her. She continues to move through the line of dangling parcels. She pulls the door at the end open wider.

There in front of her are a series of sacks also hanging from hooks. These clearly contain larger animals; she can see the shapes. They swing slightly in the darkness. Her heart has started to race. She turns and flinches; something has brushed against her. Behind her hanging down from a hook is a large sack. The bottom is unfastened as if it has only recently been put there and in a hurry. She can hardly bear to lift the bottom of the sack. LAWRENCE *is hanging by his feet from the hook. He is dead. His throat has been cut.*

ANNE *lets out an involuntary cry. She puts her hands round the sack for one moment, cradling it. Then she pulls hard on the sack, and* LAWRENCE*'s body falls into her arms. They both crash to the floor. She holds him really tight, clutching his face, touching his cheeks, as the other sacks sway slightly on their hooks around her.*

She can hear a voice calling: 'Miss Keyes . . . Miss Keyes . . . '

She has to leave him. She moves back through the hideous room full of the dangling brown parcels and out into the yard. She looks around her: there is no other exit – to get out she has to go back through the surgery.

INT. LITTLE ROOM / VET'S LOBBY. DAY.

We cut to ANNE *picking up the cages with the two cats in the little room. She moves into the lobby. The* VET *is there with*

MISS CROWLEY. *The small dog is still chained to the wall.*
There is only one person left in the queue.

ANNE: I've changed my mind . . . I am not ready to do
this . . .
She is trying her utmost to conceal her fear, but she can
feel it showing.
Thank you for giving me time to reconsider . . .
She starts to leave, holding the two cages.
THE VET: We must call you a taxi Miss Keyes, you can't
manage like that . . .
But ANNE *is moving with the two cages out on to the*
common as briskly as she can without actually running.
She is acutely conscious of them standing in the doorway
watching her go. MISS CROWLEY *is calling after her.*
MISS CROWLEY: Miss Keyes . . . !

EXT. THE COMMON. DAY.
We cut to ANNE *struggling with the two cages along a track of*
the common; she is now trying to move as fast as she can. There
are trees and thick bushes all around her, she can no longer be
seen from the surgery. She can see one of the bonfires directly
ahead of her, with the smoke pouring high and causing a pall
over the area. Two men in overalls are standing throwing sacks
on to the fire from a horrible pile next to them.

ANNE *puts down the cages. She is sweating and extremely*
scared. She realises she is not going to get very far carrying the
cats. She opens the cages.

ANNE: You two . . . go on, go . . . You are not safe with me.
The cats looking at her.
Horatio . . . Bombardier . . . *Go!*
The cats disappear into the trees. ANNE *can hear the*
sound of a vehicle coming along the track somewhere

*behind her. She moves into the bushes and along another
path, trying to keep out of sight. Right in front of her is a
second bonfire. Another man is disposing of sacks. She sees
him struggling to lift a large sack, larger than the ones of
cats and dogs. She stares at it in horror. The sack splits
open as the man tries to heave it on to the fire: the head of
a pig is visible.*

In the distance through the haze of smoke ANNE *suddenly
glimpses the man in the dark city suit on a bicycle – the
same man she saw at the church. For a moment he pauses,
staring through the smoke but not seeing her, then
continues to cycle along the path.*

ANNE *turns to move on when she sees through the trees a
vehicle coming along a track which runs close to where she
is. It is still a little distance away, an old truck lumbering
towards her. She crouches down among the bushes.*

The sound of the truck is getting louder and closer.

*Suddenly she realises she is being watched; a twelve-
year-old girl is standing staring down at her. Their eyes
meet.*

ANNE: Can you do something for me?

The girl continues to stare at her. ANNE *takes the envelope
from her bag.*

ANNE: Will you post this for me? I'll give you money, it
needs a stamp – you'll buy a stamp for it?

The girl nods and takes the money.

Here have some more . . .

The girl hesitates and then takes more money.

It's really urgent – go on, do it as soon as you can!
Please!

*The girl runs off with the envelope; she disappears down
the path, dodging through the smoke from the bonfire.*

The truck is almost level with ANNE *now, its engine
noise loud.* ANNE *lies down flat, pressing herself into the
ground. She can hear the sound of children on the common,*

*the noise of the animals burning on the bonfire, the sound
of men's voices. She turns her head, she can see through
the bushes the truck getting very close; it is being driven
by* MISS CROWLEY. *It is carrying some more sacks. The
truck stops, the engine is switched off.*

A figure gets out of the passenger seat. It is ANNE's
father.

ALEXANDER (*calling*): Anne? Where are you?

    ANNE *presses herself to the ground, a voice behind her says
'Here she is!' She looks up; the* VET *is standing peering
down at her.*

EXT. OUTSIDE THE VETERINARY SURGERY. DAY.
We cut to ANNE *sitting on the grass outside the vet's surgery.*
ALEXANDER *is sitting on the grass opposite her. If she turns her
head* ANNE *can see the outbuilding where* LAWRENCE's *body is
and if she looks the other way she can see the bonfires burning
on the common and the column of smoke.*

    ALEXANDER *is looking at her calmly, a warm look in his
eyes.* MISS CROWLEY *is approaching them with a tray of
drinks and biscuits.*

MISS CROWLEY: I thought a little home-made lemonade
    would do the trick. I knew she was upset. People do
    find it distressing . . .

    ALEXANDER *takes the lemonade but* ANNE *refuses hers.*

    I'll just leave it here then, shall I?

    MISS CROWLEY *moves off.* ANNE *staring towards the
outbuilding where* LAWRENCE *is and then back at her
father.*

ANNE: Why are you here?

ALEXANDER: They found your number on the form and
    then phoned me and said you were distraught, and
    then when I got here you had gone running out with

the cats on to the common. Why did you come right
out here, darling? To this place?

ANNE (*very quiet*): I don't know . . . I couldn't bear doing it
near home . . . (*Looks across at the common.*) I let them
go, God knows what will happen to them.

ALEXANDER: You let them go? Well, why not?

*He follows her gaze towards the bonfires and the sacks
being burnt.*

It's terrible – look what's happened in a few days! It's
like a vision of hell, isn't it? Animals going on to the
fire in a quiet English suburb . . . the world's gone
mad. (*He looks at her intensely.*) People are finding out
what war really means.

The VET *is coming towards them carrying a leather
briefcase.*

   ANNE *watching him approach, unable to conceal her
fear.*

ANNE: Why is he coming over here? (*Suddenly.*) Don't let
that man hurt me . . .

ALEXANDER: Why would he hurt you, darling?

The VET *veers off on to another path across the common
and waves.*

THE VET: Everything all right? Just going to get some more
supplies . . .

ALEXANDER (*taking out a hip flask*): Maybe we need
something stronger than lemonade!

He unscrews the flask and lifts it up. ANNE *can't stop
staring at the* VET *as he moves away. She turns back as
her father is offering her the drink. She drinks from the
flask.*

ANNE: Are you aware what they are doing? (*Her voice very
quiet.*) They are doing something awful . . .

ALEXANDER: Who, darling?

ANNE*'s voice is slurring. The picture is darkening.* ANNE
looks at her father.

ANNE: Are you doing it too?

The picture abruptly fades into black.

INT. OLD HOUSE. IN CARTER LANE. EVENING.

There is a point of light in the blackness. We are close on ANNE's eyes; they flicker, trying to open. There is the sound of very loud bells from St Paul's, harsh and loud. ANNE's eyes open. She is lying in a bed in the dark wood-panelled room in the old house under the shadow of the cathedral. The same room we saw the old men in at the beginning of the film. The shutters are closed on the windows, evening light just visible through the cracks.

   ANNE *is lying in a simple white nightdress. Her body is still heavy, her vision blurred.* RALPH *and* CELIA *are staring down at her, their voices seem to come from a long way away.*

CELIA: My darling, you are back with us.

RALPH: This noise doesn't help, does it? (*Turning towards the cacophony of bells.*) It's just somebody's wedding . . . (*He mimics.*) The bells, the bells! (*He looks at her.*) You're in Aunt Elizabeth's house . . .

ANNE (*her voice still slurring*): I thought it was shut up . . . Aunt Elizabeth's house?

RALPH: Our home is being used for other things.

   There is a noise in the corner of the room. A severe-looking woman of about sixty-five is sitting knitting in the corner. This is Mrs Knight. She will be looking after you.

   ANNE *half closes her eyes as the bells ring out. She opens them a second later.*

   CELIA *and* RALPH *are gone.* MRS KNIGHT *has stopped knitting and is just staring at her.*

   ANNE *stares back.*

EXT. ST PAUL'S. DUSK.
We see a low angle shot of St Paul's at dusk. The bells have
stopped.

INT. OLD HOUSE. DUSK.
ANNE's *eyes are open again. There is a sharp cut, showing* MRS
KNIGHT *sitting closer to the bed now. She is just staring at*
ANNE *as if she is keeping vigil. There is no sign of her knitting.*
Her eyes are very hard, very watchful. Seeing ANNE *is stirring,*
she leans forward slightly.

We move in on ANNE. *She senses she has been drugged and*
she tries to fight out of it, but it is hitting her in waves. As the
camera moves closer to her, we hear the sound of the country,
laughter and music.

There is a sudden cut to RALPH, CELIA *and* ANNE *moving*
through the abbey, warm laughter, RALPH *brandishing an*
imaginary sword calling 'Fat men dancing'.

We hear ANNE's *voice, hushed but heartfelt, over the image*
as RALPH *smiles at her.*

ANNE (*voice-over*): How could you have done that? Used
    our childhood stories . . . ?
    And then we see the shot moving round the pillar, the one
    that faded to black at the beginning of the film. Now it
    moves round the pillar to reveal RALPH *and* CELIA *staring*
    at ANNE, *their attitude completely different, as if they*
    really don't know her. They are extremely detached, while
    behind them the men in dark suits are digging and
    burying sacks and the foxtrot is playing. RALPH *turns*
    and greets the men, shakes hands with them, mingles with
    them. CELIA *looks back at* ANNE. *Then we hear voices*
    whispering about ANNE.
        'No, she is adopted of course . . . ' 'She's the eldest but
    she is the one they adopted.'

We hear ANNE*'s voice, heartfelt again, as* RALPH *and*
CELIA *are moving away from her.*

ANNE: Where are you going?

Then we see an image of RALPH *standing at the end of
the bed in the darkened room, staring straight at her. His
manner is very confident but his voice is distant.*

RALPH: Don't you realise we want people to feel defeated?!
To feel there's no hope?! That way we can do our deal
with the Germans.

ANNE*'s eyes flash open from the dream. It is night now.
It is almost pitch black.*

She hears a noise in the blackness.

Suddenly she is terrified to see MRS KNIGHT *looming
up over her, holding a cushion as if she is about to smother
her. She is staring at* ANNE *with piercing, cold eyes.*

ANNE *screams at her.*

ANNE: Get out of here! Get away from me!

*Suddenly the room is full of shadows as if other people
have entered but she can't see who they are. The image
fades to black fast.*

A match is struck. ANNE*'s eyes open again. It is still
dark but there is a little light coming through the shutters
as if it is nearly dawn.* ALEXANDER *is sitting in a corner
of the room lighting a cigarette.* ANNE *stares across at him.*

ANNE (*softly*): What is happening to me?

ALEXANDER: This is just so you can rest, dear . . . You have
been ill. You must get better.

ANNE *turns with difficulty. She realises she must have been
drugged again somehow. The room looks hallucinatory to
her, distorted. She tries to lift her body but she can't.*

ANNE (*softly*): Are they poisoning me?

ALEXANDER: Poisoning you? Of course not, darling. That
would never happen . . .

He looks across at her. He is at the other end of the room.

I can still remember when I held you for the first

time . . . when you arrived to be with us, a bundle . . .
the most perfect bundle that was ever delivered to
the house. You came in a taxi with a nurse . . . It was
raining that night and you got wet. When I held you
and felt you heavy in my arms, it was the most
beautiful present . . . I could never let harm come
to that.

ANNE (*very quiet*): So you loved me then?

ALEXANDER: Then? I love you. (*He stares at her, softly.*)
I love you still. Always. Why do you think you are
here . . .

EXT. ST PAUL'S. DAY.
*The bells suddenly explode loudly. We cut to an exterior of St
Paul's, which is seen from an angle which gives it an oppressive
quality, making the building appear strangely malevolent. The
bells are rasping out.*

EXT. OLD HOUSE. DAY.
*We cut back to the dark, panelled room. The shutters are still
closed, but bright sunlight is bursting through into the room,
casting long shadows on to the floor.*

ANNE *sits up with a start. Sitting on a chair, facing her, is*
BALCOMBE.

The shock makes ANNE's *mind race. She pulls herself up in
the bed.*

BALCOMBE: I thought you would never wake up.

ANNE: I wish I hadn't.

BALCOMBE *stares at her tray of untouched food by the bed
and then looks straight at* ANNE.

BALCOMBE: Not eating your food I see.

ANNE *refuses to look at him.*

BALCOMBE: Your father asked me to pay you a visit.

ANNE: My father . . . ? I don't believe you.

BALCOMBE: Of course, he and I are working together, have
been for a long time. Your father is a very influential
person . . . charmingly absent-minded, but very, very
influential. (*He looks across at her.*) He hides his true
seriousness my dear, except from those of us who
really know him.

BALCOMBE produces ANNE*'s envelope with the record
addressed to Winston Churchill. The one she tried to post.*
This recording of our meeting was made for him, of
course.

ANNE *stares at him holding the record.*

I am sure you knew that, my dear, or possibly you
didn't . . . All these records were for him. Why else
would they have been stored at your house? Maybe
you tried to wish it away, the obvious explanation . . .
His dark eyes watching her. ANNE *tries to meet his
piercing stare.*

It's a little hot isn't it . . .

*Suddenly he takes off his jacket and puts it on the chair,
as if he is preparing for something.* ANNE *pulls herself up
even further in the bed.* BALCOMBE *moves up to her, stares
down at her.*

The facts are these . . . because I am sure you would
like to deal just in facts, wouldn't you, Anne?

ANNE *staring at him, not replying.*

There is a group of us who believe this war against
Hitler is utter folly and who are determined to bring
it to an end. We are acting without the government's
knowledge, but we will present them with a plan when
we are ready. We are using your house in London
for a series of meetings. Your father is chairing those
meetings. That is why you are here.

He stares down at her, his eyes fixed on her.
How simple it is, and how very important.
ANNE *suddenly notices there is a drink sitting for her
on the bedside table. Then she stares defiantly back at*
BALCOMBE. BALCOMBE'S *dark eyes meet her gaze.
He twists the envelope with the gramophone record round
in his hands. There is silence.*

ANNE (*calmly*): Are you going to kill me?

BALCOMBE: My dear, what sort of question is that? Even
    for an actress! The adopted daughter of my old friend,
    what could have given you such an idea . . . ?

    BALCOMBE *moves slowly round the bed. He moves the
    drink on her bedside table precisely six inches towards her.*
    Then he stares down at her.
    We track in on the drink.
    We cut to ANNE. *And then back to* BALCOMBE, *a low
    angle shot, his powerful face staring down.*
    *The image cuts to black. Out of the blackness there is
    a loud scrabbling noise and then the sound of the shutter
    being yanked open. The room floods with a blinding shaft
    of sunlight. The figure turns from the window.*
    It is OLD WALTER. *We have cut back to the present.*

INT. THE OLD HOUSE. THE PRESENT. DAY.
We cut to MICHAEL *very nervously staring at the two old men.*
OLIVER *is watching from the corner,* WALTER *moves from the
window over to the old radio and switches it off.*

MICHAEL: What happened to her?

WALTER: You think we know?

MICHAEL: Yes, I think you do. (*Very insistent.*) You *said* you
    would tell me.

OLIVER: You really think we know what they did to her?

WALTER: Or she did to herself . . .

> MICHAEL *meets the beady stare of the two old men. He is trying not to show how scared he is.*

MICHAEL: Yes, I believe you do know . . .

> MICHAEL *suddenly notices the photographs on the wall again, the picture of St Paul's, this time not looking such a reassuring place, the child's drawing of the Fat Knight, the baby in the pushchair. He looks straight back at* WALTER's *eyes.*

MICHAEL: Tell me.

> *The bells start ringing again from the cathedral. We move in on* WALTER's *face.*

INT. OLD HOUSE. THE PAST. EVENING.

We cut back to ANNE's *face being washed with a flannel. We see* CELIA *is gently washing it. There is a bowl of warm water by the bed. The bells stop suddenly.*

CELIA: You are a little feverish, aren't you, darling, I think? Hot and cold flushes . . . you've got a temperature.

ANNE: Mr Balcombe was here.

ALEXANDER: Darling you are mistaken. Mr Balcombe was not here . . .

> ANNE *looks up. Her father is standing in the corner.*

ALEXANDER: I would never let him come back . . .

CELIA: We don't need to see that spooky man ever again . . .

> CELIA's *manner is as flighty and as relaxed as always, carrying on as if everything was completely normal.* ANNE *stares at her, wondering how much, if anything,* CELIA *has admitted to herself.*

CELIA: It's so quiet, isn't it? All the children being sent away from this part of the city . . . no children and no pets! It is the most peculiar thing, the silence out

there . . . (*She laughs.*) except for the horrid bells . . .
but then they are talking of stopping all the bells
ringing until the end of the war . . . Talk about a silver
lining! That would be simply marvellous . . . (*She
stares down at her sister.*) And you look beautiful, darling.
(*She moves.*) Now we have to find you something
delightful to eat . . .

ANNE: I am not eating anything until you stop putting
something else in it.

CELIA *turns, giving* ANNE *a bewildered look, as if she
doesn't understand.*

*For a moment she stands in the doorway and then she is
gone.*

ANNE *and* ALEXANDER *are alone.*

ANNE: Mr Balcombe *was* here. I didn't dream it. (*Staring
at her father.*) He had Lawrence killed.

ALEXANDER: You are feverish my dear . . .

ANNE (*with real force*): You did let him come back. You let
that man come and see me. How could you have
done that?

ALEXANDER *sits at the end of the bed; he looks very
elegant. He takes her hand.*

ALEXANDER: This war is a terrible thing, my dear . . . As you
know, I hate exaggeration, but everything we believe
in, everything *I* believe in, democracy, culture, art –
(*He smiles.*) all those sort of things, civilisation itself in
fact my dear, will be destroyed if we get involved in
this ruinous war. I certainly don't sympathise with the
Nazi ideology, in fact I rather despise it, but there is
absolutely no chance of us winning this war. We will
be completely destroyed unless we make peace.
Everything we value most will have gone. And we are
working to arrange that peace very hard, nothing
must disturb that . . . so things are complicated,

darling, just at the moment. Ralph understands this,
Celia understands it in her own way, but somehow
I knew you wouldn't . . . so we have to keep you here.

ANNE: To do what with?

ALEXANDER (*softly*): To keep you safe . . .

ANNE (*with force*): And this is how you keep me safe, is it?!
Their eyes meet.
You lied to me . . . all the time. About everything.

ALEXANDER (*very quiet*): Not everything . . . I couldn't
share certain things with you, what I need to do for
this country.
ALEXANDER *stares down at her. There are tears in his eyes.*
Maybe there are two sorts of love. I don't want to be
made to choose . . .

EXT. SMALL GARDEN. DAY.
We cut to the garden of the old house. MAUD *is pruning away
in the tiny, ancient garden, tending the plants. Her face
seemingly content, she is in a world of her own.*

INT. THE ROOM AT THE OLD HOUSE. DAY.
ANNE *is moving around the room in the old house, pulling at
the door, shouting to be let out, rattling at the shutters. She
yanks really hard on one of the shutters and manages to get it
open. She sees her mother below, pruning in the garden.*
*She can't get the window open, but she yells and bangs. Her
mother doesn't look up, doesn't hear her.*
ANNE*'s head turns; she hears a sound outside her door on the
landing. She bangs on the door and calls to be let out. There is
no reply. She looks through the keyhole. She can see*
ALEXANDER, CELIA *and* RALPH *in conversation together on the
stairs. They are smiling and relaxed together, though they are
deep in discussion. Her father gives* CELIA *a hug as they talk.*

RALPH *moves closer to her door, and suddenly* ANNE *can hear what they are saying.*

CELIA: Papa . . .

ALEXANDER: What?

CELIA: I have arranged another outing.

ALEXANDER: Another one?

CELIA: It is going to be wonderful, and I need you . . .

ALEXANDER (*interrupting* CELIA): You've turned into a
    proper hostess, you have, when I wasn't looking. Ralph
    can go.

CELIA: Ralph has already agreed to go.

RALPH: I am already going.

ALEXANDER: Somebody has to be here for Anne, we have
    to monitor the situation very closely.

RALPH: Well, nobody would ever listen to Anne anyway,
    she's got no evidence, but it is best we do this . . . We
    can handle her, come on! It's simple, we will bring
    Mrs Knight back, it's the best solution because Mrs
    Knight will get something down her which will keep
    her completely quiet. Sedated for days and days.
    We are on ANNE's *eye as it stares through the keyhole and
    then we see the close body language of her siblings and her
    father. The image slows for a moment as we see them so
    intimate together and unconcerned, even though she is
    imprisoned just a few feet away.*
        *We cut back to her eye, and then we hear this
    extraordinary noise come out of* ANNE, *a deep guttural
    voice.*

ANNE: You fucking bastards!
    RALPH, CELIA *and* ALEXANDER *turn, startled, towards
    the door.*
    You fucking people . . . you are nothing to do with me!
    We cut to RALPH, ALEXANDER *and* CELIA *entering the
    room; we move with them. We are greeted by the sight of*

ANNE *standing right at the other end of the room in her*
nightdress, her body strong, full of rage and power; her tone
is not hysterical though, it is full of authority. But her
voice is entirely different.

You are not going to bring that ghastly woman back
here . . . You think I am going to let that bitch look
after me? I am not going to let that fucking woman
terrorise me . . .

They stare at her, completely stunned by her.

Why are you looking like that? I don't see why you
should be surprised! I am not frightened of you fucking
people! Remember I am the daughter of gypsies and it
was bound to come out sooner or later – what I 'really
am' – that's what you think isn't it? Well, here it is!
You think you could scare me into silence, you
fucking bastards . . . I am not afraid of you – you'll
have to do better than that! If you are going to do
anything you'll have to do it yourself.

ALEXANDER (*very quiet*): Darling . . .

ANNE: Don't you fucking darling me, you bastard. *You are*
nothing to do with me.

    There is complete silence. They stare at her.

RALPH (*quiet*): This is not the way, Glorious . . . it really
isn't! (*To* ALEXANDER *and* CELIA.) Just leave me alone
with her.

    RALPH *stares across at* ANNE. *They are alone.*

    Then RALPH *slams the shutter tight shut again on the*
window.

Why don't you ever do what you are told? . . . Why do
you insist you always know best?! Because, in the end,
what you never realised was – you knew *nothing*.
Nothing that really mattered! (*He stares at her, fury in*
his eyes.) And you just wouldn't listen to me, would
you . . . ! I told you to get on with your life. And now
look what's happened to you . . . (*Their eyes meet.*) We

just have to stop giving you water, Glorious, and it's all over . . .

The door crashes shut and the lock is turned. We hear the sound of RALPH, CELIA *and* ALEXANDER *leaving. A shot of* ANNE *standing alone in the shuttered room.*

A high shot of the room. It is dusk now. We hear the sound of an air raid siren.

We move in on ANNE's *face.*

We cut to RALPH *and* CELIA *and* ANNE *on the terrace of the Norfolk house: their intense closeness. We move around their faces.*

We cut back to ANNE; *there are tears on her cheeks. The light has changed. It is morning.* ANNE *is already weaker. We hear a bluebottle buzzing in the room.*

We cut to ANNE's *face and then we cut to her father holding her tight in his arms and saying softly:*

ALEXANDER: I'll never let you go away again . . .

We cut back to ANNE. *She lets out a silent cry. The light has changed again. The room is streaked with evening sun. There is the sound of a cat mewing.* ANNE *stumbles across to the window; we see how weak she is. She can hear the sound of the cat loudly on the other side of the shutter. She looks through the crack and sees Bombardier. We see a close-up of the cat staring at* ANNE *caged in the room through the crack in the shutter.*

ANNE *is too weak to open the shutter.*

ANNE: Bombardier . . . you can't get in . . . and I can't get out.

The sound of another air raid warning, really loud and close.

INT. OLD LONDON HOUSE, RECEPTION ROOM. 1939.
We dissolve into a very high shot staring down at ANNE, *her body stretched out on the bed. The air raid siren turns into bells,*

loud, rasping bells as the shot tracks down towards ANNE's
body, the bells increasing in volume all the time. ANNE *is lying
very still.*

We cut for a fleeting moment to OLD WALTER *and* OLIVER
in the same room in the present, staring at MICHAEL.

We cut back to ANNE. *The bells have stopped for a moment;
there is total silence as she lies curled tight and still on the bed.*

Then very faintly we can hear the sound of children. ANNE
*stirs. She gets up in her nightdress, barefoot. The sound of the
children's voices grows a little louder.*

She shouts out.

ANNE: Anyone there?

> *She pulls at the door half-heartedly, expecting to find it
> locked as always, but the door swings open.*
>
> ANNE *moves with difficulty out on to the landing. In
> front of her are a pair of shiny men's shoes sitting neatly
> at the top of the stairs. She puts them on, sitting on the
> staircase, doing the laces up as quickly as she can; at first
> her fingers won't move fast enough. The children's voices
> are getting louder all the time.*

EXT. CARTER LANE AND SURROUNDS. DAY.
ANNE *comes out of the house and into the little hidden square
in the nightdress and the black shoes. Her mother is there,
tending the plants in the little front garden.*

ANNE: Mama, did you open the door?

> MAUD *has her back to her as she bends over the flowers.
> She turns and stares at* ANNE *with nervous eyes and a
> frightened smile.*

Thank you, Mama . . .

> MAUD *stares at her daughter for a moment and then she
> speaks in an urgent whisper.*

MAUD: Go . . . !

*MAUD's eyes are imploring ANNE to go while she still can.
ANNE meets her mother's look, gives her a little nod and
moves off in her nightdress and her black shoes.*

*We cut to her moving along the alleyway near the
cathedral. We can hear the sound of the children really
loud. A figure is standing at the end of the alleyway with
his back to her. He turns; it is YOUNG WALTER.*

YOUNG WALTER: Anne . . . what are you doing?

ANNE: I need to get away from here, Walter.

YOUNG WALTER: Come this way . . . I will find you a taxi.

ANNE hesitates. She is very weak.

I will . . .

*The sound of the children in front of them is loud and very
close.*

ANNE (*softly*): Who are those children . . . ? I thought all
the children had been evacuated from round here.

YOUNG WALTER: They have . . . (*Beckoning to her.*) Come
this way. (*He walks by her side.*) Tell me what's happened
to you, Anne . . .

*We cut to ANNE and YOUNG WALTER coming out of the
alley by some railings.*

*Beyond the railings is a small park which lies very near
St Paul's. The camera cranes up gently over the railings
and reveals some of the young children that were at the
ambassadors' party, playing.*

*Beyond them are ALEXANDER, CELIA and RALPH,
standing watching the children play. And sitting in the
shadows of a tree is AUNT ELIZABETH. They all look up,
seeing ANNE in her nightdress staring at them through the
railings.*

YOUNG WALTER has led her back to all of them.

YOUNG WALTER: There they are . . . you can join your
family, Anne.

ANNE *stares at them through the railings. She cannot move. Despite everything the pull towards her family is still strong.*

AUNT ELIZABETH (*calling across*): Come and join us, Anne.

ALEXANDER (*staring back at her*): Anne . . . come here darling . . . come to me . . .

The bells from the cathedral are ringing out loudly.

We move in on ANNE *as she stands staring at them by the railings. Her father beckons to her again, lifting his arms. Their eyes meet.*

Suddenly she turns and starts running, running as fast as she can.

YOUNG WALTER *watches her go.*

We see her figure disappearing in her white nightdress into the darkness, getting smaller and smaller.

INT. THE OLD HOUSE. THE PRESENT. AFTERNOON.
We cut back to WALTER *and* OLIVER *in the present. The same bells are ringing out loudly.* WALTER *and* OLIVER *both stare at* MICHAEL *out of the darkness.*

WALTER: And none of us saw her again.

OLIVER: None of us!

WALTER: She died in Canada, I believe, about twenty years ago.

OLIVER: Of course they didn't really starve her, did they? She went on a hunger strike . . .

WALTER: It's what she told me as we walked along that last day . . . (*Blithely.*) But it was her love of the dramatic, no doubt! One will never know of course . . .

OLIVER: Because we are the only ones left.

OLIVER *suddenly reaches up and closes the shutter again. The clock on St Paul's chimes five o'clock.*

WALTER: I've tried to be honest, told you everything.

He searches for MICHAEL's *reaction.*

No words of condemnation . . . for me?

MICHAEL (*a pause, staring down at the family album*): No, you were very young, after all . . .

OLIVER: I was a baby! And it was such a long time ago. Nobody remembers!

WALTER: I just did what they wanted . . .

We begin to move in on his eyes.

What Mr Balcombe and *the family* wanted. They told me she needed to be taught a lesson . . .

We see a sudden flashback. BALCOMBE *whispering to the* YOUNG WALTER *on the edge of the wood.* RALPH *watching from the shadows. And then we see* YOUNG WALTER *moving the* YOUNG OLIVER *in the pushchair as* ANNE *sleeps at the picnic. We see him disappear into the wood with the pushchair.*

And then we see him watching fascinated through the leaves as ANNE *begins to search frantically for the baby. Suddenly there is a movement behind him; he turns.* AUNT ELIZABETH *is standing next to him, watching* ANNE. *She bends down to whisper in his ear approvingly.*

AUNT ELIZABETH: So you managed to move the baby without her seeing!

YOUNG WALTER (*smiles*): Oh yes.

We cut back to the present, to WALTER's *face.*

WALTER: I did what I thought was right . . .

We stay on his eyes, we see he is troubled by the memory, haunted by it.

Is twelve too young to know right from wrong?

He moves his hand as if swatting away the past, as if he has reassured himself.

I was only doing what was expected. It was a very strange time back then . . . And I had even tried to warn her . . .

MICHAEL, *who has been watching him carefully, glances down at the photos of* ANNE *in the album. He pauses for a moment at the picture of* CELIA, *his grandmother.*
   He looks concerned.

OLIVER (*watching this*): They've all gone now! . . . Can't trouble us! Can't trouble Walter . . .
   WALTER *nods. It is very dark in the room.*

MICHAEL: Yes . . . (*He shuts the album.*) I must go . . . (*He begins to move.*) There is just one thing, a little favour . . .

WALTER: Another one?

MICHAEL: My mother arranged to meet me round here, she will have been waiting for a little while now. It's very close by. If you can just come and say hello, I know she will appreciate it. She didn't want to come here, to the house, I expect you understand –

WALTER: She should have come with you. Why didn't she?

MICHAEL: I did try to persuade her. But I am not sure she wanted to hear it all first hand . . . but she would like to meet you. I believe it's years since you've seen her . . . Please will you come?

EXT. ALLEYWAY / PARK. AFTERNOON.
We cut to MICHAEL *leading the two old men down through the maze of dark alleyways near the cathedral. The old men walk with difficulty.*
   MICHAEL *beckons to them as* YOUNG WALTER *did.*
   They move out of the labyrinth of the alleyways and find themselves by the railings of the small park. The old men shuffling behind MICHAEL.
   There is no one in the park, just empty benches, some old gravestones in the corner.
   The three of them stand for a moment staring across at the ancient little park under the shadow of St Paul's.

WALTER: So where is your mother?

MICHAEL: She will be here . . .

The sound of the wind through the tall trees.

And then we move in on WALTER's *face; he is transfixed with real horror. Out of the shadows, beneath the trees a figure is being wheeled towards them. We see the wheels of the wheelchair crunch on the gravel. We catch a glimpse of the elderly figure through the trees. For a terrifying moment it is* AUNT ELIZABETH *staring back from the wheelchair.*

We cut to WALTER's *face, fearful like a child.*

WALTER: It's not possible . . .

The figure keeps coming, half glimpsed through the trees. AUNT ELIZABETH *bearing down on him, her powerful stare straight into his eyes. The past won't let go of him.*

WALTER's *voice is hushed with fear; he answers the stare of the approaching figure.*

WALTER: I didn't mean to tell him everything . . . Forgive me. (*Very hushed.*) I won't tell anyone else . . .

We cut to MICHAEL *watching* WALTER *closely as the figure approaches.*

The old woman is being pushed by Michael's mother and is relentlessly coming towards them.

As she gets nearer we see it is not AUNT ELIZABETH *but a very old woman who looks different. For a moment immense relief appears on* WALTER's *face. But the figure is still bearing down on him through the shadows of the trees like an avenging ghost. The past is alive and coming straight at him. We are on* WALTER's *eyes, suddenly tense again. The figure reaches them.*

MICHAEL: Walter, Oliver, this is my mother . . . and this –

He indicates the old lady.

– is Anne Keyes.

The two old men stare at ANNE. *They are stunned, frightened and a little humbled.*

OLD ANNE: It's good to meet you, gentlemen, it's so very good.

WALTER: Anne . . . I had no idea! No idea at all!

OLD ANNE (*smiles*): No idea I was still here . . . No, I know you didn't.

WALTER (*to* MICHAEL, *very disquieted*): So you knew all along?

OLIVER: You knew!

> MICHAEL *looks at* ANNE *and then back at the old men.*

MICHAEL: We wanted to hear it from your own lips . . .

> *The two old men are backing away, very nervous, as if they can't cope with the stare of the old lady. They seem to shrivel in front of her.*
>
> *The bells start chiming from St Paul's.*

OLD ANNE: I just wanted to say hello again.

> *She lifts her head and stares straight at them.*

Since we are *family* . . .

> *We move in on the old lady's face as the bells ring out. Her face gradually dissolves into the face of* ANNE *in her youth staring directly out at us.*